BADMINTON
Revisited

BADMINTON
Revisited
AN ANECDOTAL HISTORY

Julian Seaman

JR
BOOKS

First published in Great Britain in 2009 by
JR Books, 10 Greenland Street, London NW1 0ND
www.jrbooks.com

A catalogue record for this book is available from the British Library.

Photography courtesy of Kit Houghton and the Badminton archives.

ISBN 978-1-906779-47-4

1 3 5 7 9 10 8 6 4 2

Printed by MPG Books, Bodmin, Cornwall

Contents

Acknowledgements

I have been a Badminton fan for over 45 years, but for the accounts of the first 15 Trials, and indeed for the more general reportage, I am indebted to five main sources. Barbara Cooper wrote the account of the first 20 years, *Badminton: A Record of the Three-Day Event from 1949 to 1969*, and encouraged me into print in 1983 with *Horse Laughs*. Debby Sly's *Badminton Horse Trials: The Triumphs And The Tears* celebrated the event's 50th anniversary. My school contemporary Rhydain Wynn-Williams compiled a comprehensive book of statistics up to 1988, by which time I was writing the rider biographies for the event and TV commentators, and doing my own research. Also the *Horse & Hound* and *Eventing* archives and my very good friends Kate Green and Julie Harding, who have covered Badminton for the magazines for over 10 years, have helped refresh my memory.

Badminton for beginners

The Badminton Horse Trials (indeed all Three Day Events) consists, as many will know, of three basic elements, which are considered the ultimate test of all round horsemanship. This is now spread over four competitive days. Until 2006 (about more later), the week would run something like this: day one, usually Wednesday, the riders were briefed in Badminton Village Hall. The endurance phases were then open for inspection by the riders on foot. In the evening is a mandatory inspection of all horses known as the trot up, to make sure they are up to the task ahead. The unfolding of the competition, in which the horse and rider endeavour to complete all elements, starts with a dressage test on either Thursday or Friday, depending on the draw. This is comparable to compulsory figures in skating, and tests the horses' suppleness, elegance and obedience. Riders usually wear top hats and tailcoats for this test. On the cross country (or endurance) day, Saturday, this same docile horse must become a fast, bold jumping machine. For many years this element included a phase A of several miles of trotting round the outer reaches of the park (known as roads and tracks) before arriving at phase B, which was a steeplechase of about 10 jumps, which horses would go round individually against the clock. It was then on to phase C, a second section of roads and tracks of several miles (the distances varied over the years) before coming into a pen where the grooms and owners would be waiting. Horses would be checked over again during a compulsory 10-minute breather before being counted down to set off round the cross country course of up to 35 solid jumps such as walls, ditches, ponds, hedges and fences covering up to 5 miles (8km). Penalties are imposed for refusals and falls. This is also timed. On the final (Sunday) morning there is another trot up for the horses still in the competition before the show jumping phase over knock down jumps. This is to test that the riders haven't taken too much out of their horses during the cross country efforts.

Preface

Badminton Horse Trials is one of the world's most famous sporting events. An all round test of horsemanship, it has been held in the Duke of Beaufort's magnificent Gloucestershire park since 1949.

The competition consists of three elements, but the most challenging is the enormous cross-country jumping course, held on the Saturday. Today, the event attracts a total crowd in the region of 200,000. For the public there is also the added attraction of over 300 tented trade stands. The Badminton Horse Trials is almost unique in that men and women have competed on an equal basis from the start.

Over the years famous winners have included Richard Meade, Mark Phillips, Mary King, Mark Todd and Pippa Funnell. Also featuring have been Princess Anne and recently her daughter Zara Phillips.

From the early 1960s one very keen spectator was your author. For eight years during the 1970s and early 1980s I realised my ambition by competing alongside the better known names, so experienced all the thrills and heartaches that this unique contest throws up.

However, I've possibly had a greater insight into the event than many of the more illustrious riders. I have also reported on it for equestrian magazines, written the form guide for *Horse & Hound*, been a TV commentator for the event, broadcast on the radio station, conducted the evening interviews with the leading riders and since 2002 have been the event's Media Officer.

In this book I alternate between a factual round-up of many of the aspects of the event over its 60-year history, and my own wry and hopefully humorous memories of the considerable number of years that Badminton has been a part of my life.

This tome isn't intended to be the definitive account of Three Day Eventing, nor is it a book for casual followers of the event. It is a personal story of Badminton written by an eventing enthusiast for eventing fans.

There may be the odd 'horsey' reference contained within, with which not all of you are familiar, but I make no apology for that. There are many nuances to our great sport – not the least of which is why Three Day Eventing takes place over four days! – which are too complex to explain here. (For a fuller assessment consult www.britisheventing.com and www.badminton-horse.co.uk) And it's probably those nuances which have made Three Day Eventing, and especially the Badminton Horse Trials, so special to us . . . since a spring day in 1949.

PART 1

THE FOUNDATIONS
(1949–1962)

The creation of Badminton, and its almost instant place in the sporting calendar, has of course been chronicled once or twice before. Although this is intended to be a history of the great event through my experiences, I was not born until 1955, six years after the inaugural Trials and have no anecdotes of the event from my infancy, or some years thereafter! It would, however, be perverse not to put my memories into the context of the 60 years of Badminton Horse Trials to date.

So how did Badminton Horse Trials arrive almost perfectly formed at a Gloucestershire park in the spring of 1949? Much has to do with the origins of the sport of eventing, which has also been known by several other names, including Combined Training, Concours Complet, Gebrauchspferdeprufungen, Horse Trials and most pertinently, the Military.

Various formats of an ultimate test of horsemanship were devised in the 19th and early 20th century cavalry schools of Europe and were later described by US Army General Tupper Cole as 'a military event based on the duty of the Officer Courier who got through or died.' The earliest report of cross-country jumping instruction is that of the Cavalry of King Charles XI of Sweden as they schooled over cross-country fences in 1688 to the instruction of the riding manual: 'When jumping a fence the rider will grab the mane, close his eyes and shout "Hey".'

The French can probably claim to have staged the first recognisable Three Day Event. In 1902 the Championnat du Cheval d'Armes was staged, for officers only. The obligatory dressage test, which was ridden on the first day, was a fairy simple one, but extra points could be gained in the optional reprise libre or freestyle. Some took this more seriously than others: suffice to say that the overall winner of this stage offered 'shoulder in, serpentines, canter on two tracks, half turns on haunches and forehand without changing pace or gait, changing the leg in four time, two time and at every stride. He also performed a piaffe on the spot and backwards and finally a backwards canter.'

Equestrian competitions, including the Three Day Event, were first included in the Stockholm Olympiad of 1912. The format was very different to the one we know today. First day was endurance and cross country, consisting of 50km (30 miles) roads and tracks and 5km (3 miles) cross country. Horses and riders had the second day off, followed by the speed day of steeplechase. Show jumping was the next day and finally the dressage test. I suspect that the order of the disciplines, if not the distances, would cause havoc with today's riders.

The two World Wars interrupted the Olympics, but in July and August 1948 London staged what became known as the Austerity Games. The British Horse Society, then based in London, held a council meeting during the winter of 1947 and decided to enter a Grand Prix Jumping team and a Three Day Event team.

Colonel Trevor Horn was asked to be one of the selectors and a Brigadier Bowden-Smith, one of very few who had any experience of this sort of competition, was put in charge as Director of the Three Day Event. Colonel Horn's involvement here is crucial to the history. This was the first Three Day Event to be held in Britain so he was ideal a year later to become the first Director of Badminton. He was asked to be area manager for the event, which was to be based at Aldershot, fittingly a military garrison. He went down a fortnight before and familiarised himself with the layout and met some of the competitors. It was completely new territory to him.

Cross country day covered a distance of 22 miles (35km) with a time of 1 hour 50 minutes to complete. The 57 riders set off at five-minute intervals, the first going at 6.00am and the last finishing at 12.30pm as organisers were worried about heat conditions. The roads and tracks took competitors to the still existing Tweseldown Racecourse for the steeplechase. (Tweseldown was where I spent many years of my formative equestrian life at Pony Club camps from the age of nine, to adult eventing then point-to-point riding, so could claim this as my earliest tentative link to inspiration for the first Badminton.) The second roads and tracks took them to the cross country at Barossa, behind the Royal Military Academy at Sandhurst, where as a child, I jumped the remnants of the course out with the Staff College Drag.

On that August morning in 1948, while serving at Sandhurst, my father was one of the curious crowd. With respect to my father, there was also a rather more influential spectator, the Vice-Patron and Vice-President of the International Equestrian Federation, who was being driven around by his friend and neighbour, Colonel Trevor Horn. It was the 10th Duke of Beaufort.

Welcome to Badminton

Though none of the British team of three – Major Peter Borwick with Liberty, Brigadier Lyndon Bolton on Sylvestre and Major Dougie Stewart riding Dark Seal – had ever seen a competition quite like it (though the British had managed bronze before the War at the Berlin Games), it was hoped that they could put up a good show, considering Britain's equestrian and hunting heritage. Sadly it was not to be. Major Borwick managed a creditable 17th place individually, but Brigadier Lyndon Bolton fell twice and Dougie Stewart had to retire with a lame horse before the cross country.

At a picnic lunch at the back of a Land Rover after watching horses negotiate the 35 obstacles, the Duke suggested to Trevor Horn that it would be a good idea if a similar competition could be run on an annual basis to train up a team for the next Olympics at Helsinki in 1952. He said that if the British Horse Society would sanction it, he would offer Badminton Park for the purpose. He also asked Trevor Horn (the new 'expert' with two weeks' experience of Horse Trials) to direct the event.

A committee was formed, which included Aldershot veteran Peter Borwick and, as Assistant Director, the splendid figure of Lt. Col. R.B.

(Babe) Moseley. The latter would emerge in the 1970s as the Chairman of the British Junior Team selectors to frighten and encourage us aspiring internationals in equal measure.

It seems odd, but there weren't really any rules for the new event, just some guidelines from the International Equestrian Federation. During the winter of 1948 Horn used the guidelines to draft some proper rules and regulations for Badminton, which were then scrutinised at British Horse Society meetings in London.

The scoring system from the start was based on penalties, with the lowest score winning.

Nowadays, with about 200 horse trials a year in Britain alone, there are scores of people adept at seeing an area of countryside and visualising a cross country course on the site. Indeed sometimes three courses of different levels on the same site. For Trevor Horn however this was something completely new. A strange anomaly is that although Great Britain has easily the largest number of horse trials in the world of all levels leading up to Badminton, it was Badminton which came first and the sport developed downwards.

With a vast park like Badminton (1,500 acres) the choice of route must have been daunting, remembering that a course for the roads and tracks and a site for the steeplechase also had to be taken into account. Horn used various forms of transport to survey the park, sometimes on a horse, sometimes on a bicycle and also driving by car round the local area. The route for the endurance day had to cover 14 miles (22km), as indeed it did for many years afterwards.

There were five separate sections of endurance in the early days: roads and tracks, steeplechase, second roads and tracks, cross country and a run in to cool the horse down. All of these had to measured. Other responsibilities included recruiting officials and finding accommodation for them and the competitors, and in a wonderful vignette of a past world, the schedule sent to the riders also stated that accommodation would also be organised for competitors' grooms and chauffeurs.

The British Horse Society

BADMINTON

3 DAYS EVENT

APRIL 20th, 21st and 22nd

1949

PROGRAMME

TWO SHILLINGS AND SIXPENCE.

Although the Estate Office helped where they could, most of the administration was handled in London by the British Horse Society Offices, with the top of Colonel Horn's piano in Gloucestershire as his director's office. (The Horse Trials Office is, of course, now in Badminton village, but I run the media office from London today.)

Much work needed doing to alert the media for that first Badminton, as nobody, even in the horse world, had any idea what this competition was all about. Its inaugural title was the Badminton Three Days Event, but the public really did confuse it with the shuttlecock game, which incidentally was invented in the hall of Badminton House. In 1951, the year before the Helsinki Olympics, for which the Trials had been instigated, the name was changed to The Olympic Horse Trials, Badminton. This was technically correct as the Event was a trial for the Olympics, but also created a muddle as the sport was also known as Horse Trials, and Badminton was not the Olympics. Eventually it became the simply titled Badminton Horse Trials in 1956.

With admirable chutzpah the posters for the first Badminton pronounced it 'The Most Important HORSE EVENT In Great Britain'. Pedestrians paid one shilling. Motors cost £1 a day or £2 10s for a season pass. Charabancs were £2 10s for 26-seaters and £3 for 30-seaters.

At the first Badminton there were 22 starters: 20 from Great Britain and two, Lt. Eddie Boylan and Ian Dudgeon, from Ireland. The first phase, the dressage, was held in front of Badminton House with straw bales as seats for the spectators. This phase was a bit of a shambles, with one or two notable exceptions. Several horses found it hard to make the corners in probably their first test in a confined arena. Others needed the strongest of control from their riders. Many of the crowd from hunting and racing backgrounds disapproved of these 'circus tricks' imposed on thoroughbreds. The more knowledgeable felt sorry for the horses for what they saw as bad riding.

Way out in front in the dressage was Capt. Tony Collings, a professional instructor, which would bar him from the Olympics, on

Remus with a score of 56. Also up there was John Shedden, another instructor, in third with strong-pulling American thoroughbred Golden Willow on 90.

April in England is notorious for fickle weather and cross country day was cold and wet. Trevor Horn's course suited a bold attacking attitude from the riders as those early jumps were big and formidable but not overcomplicated. By today's standard the timber used to construct the jumps, built by the Badminton head forester Mr Chappell, would be considered flimsy and therefore less inviting than jumps made with the massive timber used today.

Considering the conditions, the course, which had been designed to replicate a good run out hunting, was best tackled at hunting pace. There were 21 obstacles, and as a hint of what was to come in later years, rider disquiet on the first walk round persuaded the organisers to modify five fences.

In the conditions eight competitors were eliminated on the course and there were several falls. However there were some copybook rounds, including the dressage leader Tony Collins and Remus, John Shedden with Golden Willow and S.C.M. Thompson and Guinea Fowl, who, as you could in the early days, reduced their dressage cricket score of 191 with bonus points to lie second overnight. Yet they would be the first of many down the years to suffer the bitter disappointment of having to withdraw on the final day after the heroics of the cross country. Right up there was one of the five lady riders, Vivien Machin-Goodall and Neptune who many years later was the scariest Pony Club instructor I ever had.

There was no crowd control and Reg Hindley and Stealaway were baulked by a spectator while in mid-air at a fence and fell on landing. They still came 11th. Another casualty who failed to complete was the redoubtable Brigadier J. Scott-Coburn, who was three-times winner of the Kadir Cup, the 'pig sticking blue riband of India'.

Clear show jumping rounds proved as elusive as they do today, a knockdown cost 10 penalties then, with only Ian Dudgeon, resplendent in top hat, posting a clean sheet. John Shedden, however, had such a commanding overnight lead that with only one fence down he went into the record books as the first winner of what indeed had been, and still is, the most important horse event in Great Britain.

Olympic Trials and European Championships

That first Badminton had a crowd of about 6,000 over the three days and made a grand profit of £20.

News had obviously spread about Badminton, because in 1950, in admittedly clement weather, about 3,000 watched the dressage, 10,000 the cross country and 6,000 the show jumping. Quoting crowd numbers, as I am now expected to do as Media Officer, is an inexact science. The 1950 figures could be read as a total of 19,000, though, as now, many of that number would have come on all three days. Nevertheless, however you read the figures it was a healthy increase on the inaugural event.

Thirty riders went to post, again mainly British but this time with three from Ireland, no doubt encouraged by Ian Dudgeon's second place the previous year. The defending champion John Shedden entered two horses, committing himself to about 30 miles (50km) of competition on the Saturday afternoon. Tony Collings, who was to be the British team trainer in lieu of a team place for himself, led the dressage by a street.

In the field that year were two officers who would become more well known in other equestrian spheres: Major John Miller, who was to become Crown Equerry, credited with encouraging Princess Anne to take up the sport, and Major Dick Hern, the legendary racehorse trainer.

This time there were 28 cross country fences including the Irish Bank, still there today. In what has become a Badminton legend, John Shedden's headstrong reigning champion, instead of conventionally touching down on the top, jumped the whole thing in one.

Tony Collings retained his lead, despite an appeal from John Shedden for his second ride Kingpin. Shedden, however, completed his marathon, coming fifth on Golden Willow.

In 1951 Badminton opened up its invitation to Continental Europe. There were 33 entries: 21 from Great Britain, two from Ireland, two from Holland and a surprising eight from Switzerland, a country with little or no cross country tradition. Also the Swiss competitors had not jumped since the previous August and had spent most of the time since then in an indoor school. Needless to say this gave them a great advantage in the dressage, but the British were confident that a fairly stiff cross country course would see their challenge off. The Swiss squad were heard to say that they weren't worried as their horses were 'obedient'.

On the cross country course was a new type of fence, known as the Coffin (something I have always thought of as a misnomer as the rail on a drop to a ditch with a slope up to a rail, more resembled a grave). This fence was the downfall of most of the British riders (and a portent of similar annihilation in 1973). The obedient Swiss horses jumped it perfectly and Hans Schwarzenbach and Vae Victis became the only Continental combination ever to win the event until Nicolas Touzaint and Hildago de L'Ile in 2008. As a footnote to 1951, another of the Swiss squad, coming 10th on Tambour, was Sam Koechlin who married Britain's first lady show jumping star, Pat Smythe.

Badminton, having been ostensibly invented as a build up to the Helsinki Games, took on a different feel in the Olympic year of 1952. If Badminton was a warm up for the Games, now there was a modest network of One Day Events, with all phases bar the endurance, as warm ups for Badminton. The sport was taking root. The cast list of 26

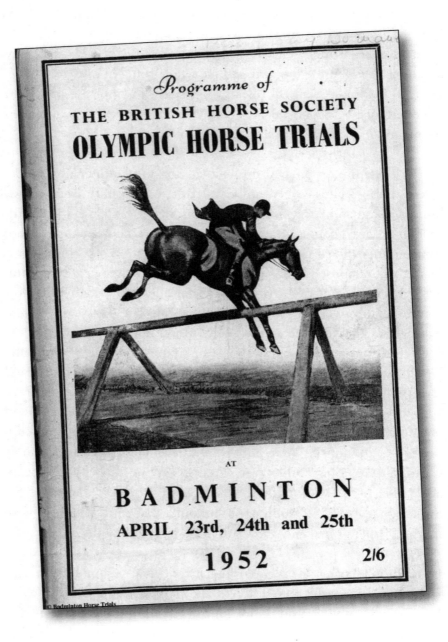

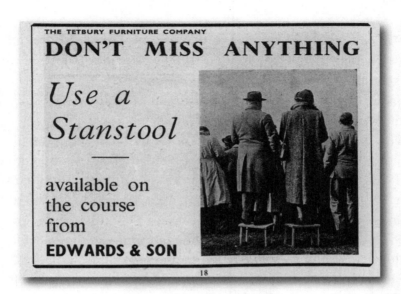

THE TETBURY FURNITURE COMPANY

DON'T MISS ANYTHING

Use a Stanstool

available on
the course
from

EDWARDS & SON

18

riders was back to just the British and Irish. In what was to become a regular cycle until quite recently, the course became increasingly difficult each year up to an Olympiad. The now famous Quarry was there for the first time. The distance was now up to 4½ miles (7km) and there were 34 fences, a distance and fence count familiar for many following years.

1952 also saw the first of what was to become a continuing connection between Badminton and the Royal Family, when the Queen attended for the first time as a guest of the Duke and Duchess of Beaufort. She retrieved the stick of a soaked Olympic hopeful, John Oram, as he emerged from a dip in the water. (In 1977 the same John Oram was given the impossible task of keeping some discipline among the group of 12 of us riders who were stunt doubles on the film *International Velvet*.)

The Queen was unable to cheer on a British victory that year, however, as the spoils went to Ireland's Capt. Mark Darley, whose ancestor's name prefixes the Darley Arabian, one of the three founts of the thoroughbred, and the diminutive mare Emily Little, descended from the same horse. 1952 also saw the first appearance at Badminton of Major Frank Weldon, whose inauspicious debut, retiring on the cross country, gave no indication of the vast contribution he would make to the sport and Badminton in particular.

Sadly the British team only managed seventh at Helsinki, but Badminton was now more than just an Olympic trial.

The sport had sufficiently taken off for the FEI, the International Equestrian Federation, to instigate a first European Championships in 1953 and Badminton was chosen as the venue. It was one of the very few times that Badminton has hosted a team event. There had been an ad hoc affair when the Swiss and Dutch had come over in 1951, but this was official. Not for the last time did the selectors not include the eventual winner (Laurence Rook and Starlight XV) in the team, but they could breathe a sigh of relief as the team of Frank Weldon (Kilbarry), Reg Hindley (Speculation) and Bertie Hill (Bambi V) became European team champions to complement Rook's individual title.

This was Trevor Horn's last year as director and he handed over the reins of a prospering annual phenomenon to his brother-in-law, Colonel Gordon Cox-Cox.

A trip to Windsor

Bambi V, who had been lent as a team horse as Olympic reserve in 1952, and retained by the squad for the victorious Europeans the following year, was returned to her owner, Margaret Hough. At this stage only male riders had been eligible for International Championship events. Margaret led the dressage, no doubt benefiting from the training Bambi had received with the British team. At least this was some consolation for selflessly giving up her horse for her kingdom.

Another lady rider, Diana Mason, was second after this phase with

14

Tramella. Diana later went on to represent Britain in pure dressage. On the cross country Margaret and Bambi had a refusal at the Luckington Lane crossing, but the horse was going very strongly and posted a good time. This was still the era of bonus points, so any jumping errors on the course could be made up. Bambi went on to win, opening a debate about the scoring system. Should a horse that had a stop on the cross country win at the expense of one with a clear round? Frank Weldon was second on Kilbarry. In fifth place was Ireland's Harry Freeman-Jackson on Brown Sugar, who had unbelievably run second in the Irish Derby the week before.

1954 was the first time Badminton was televised by the BBC and has been ever since.

The first World Championships weren't inaugurated until 1966, so between Olympics the sport held consecutive Europeans. The first had been at Badminton in 1953 then went to Basle in Switzerland the following year. In 1955 they were again awarded to Great Britain, and therefore nominally to Badminton. The Queen, however, had become an enthusiast for this developing equestrian sport and offered Windsor Great Park as the venue.

Somewhat bizarrely this Windsor Event is considered as Badminton on an awayday, and forms part of the Badminton records. From 1979 to 2006 Windsor ran its own Three Day Event for which Princess Anne was President.

The 1955 competition should really be termed an 'open' European Championships as there were also riders from Australia, Canada and South Africa. There was a fairly large field of 53 competitors from nine countries fielding five teams. The rules had been changed so that now the teams consisted of four combinations, with the best three scores to count. Representing Great Britain were Diana Mason and Tramella, Frank Weldon on Kilbarry, Laurence Rook with Starlight and Bertie Hill and Countryman III. Tramella was eliminated on the cross country, Countryman had one stop at the sandpit but made up time to take individual bronze. Non-team-member, the aforementioned Naval Lt. Commander John Oram took individual silver. Equestrian competition was all part and parcel of Army life, but Oram's achievement was remarkable for a Navy officer. The title went to Frank Weldon on the increasingly consistent Kilbarry.

Only two teams completed the competition intact, with Great Britain taking gold followed by the Swiss. One of the joys of poring over record books is spotting names from a different context. In seventh place, for Sweden was Capt. The Baron Hans von Blixen-Finecke, whose relative was Karen Blixen of *Out of Africa* fame.

If Frank Weldon had realised his potential, coming an unheralded 13th was a young girl riding in her first Three Day Event, Sheila Willcox on High and Mighty. She wasn't to be unheralded for long.

After Windsor, Countryman, which Bertie Hill had owned, was bought by a syndicate of the Queen, the Queen Mother, Colonel, V.D.S. Williams (father of commentator Dorian) and the Duke of Beaufort. Bertie kept the ride.

1956 was another Olympic year. The main summer Games were in Melbourne but both the distance and quarantine laws made equestrian competition impractical there so they were relocated to Stockholm. If the equestrian world wasn't going to go to Australia, nothing would deter the Australians coming to Europe, and there were no fewer than seven entered for Badminton that year. With two entries, Radar and Dandy, was Brian Crago, who eventually settled in Britain, just up the road from Tweseldown Racecourse. Brian became principal trainer to subsequent British world championships' bronze medallist, Olympic rider, Badminton runner up and fourth director of the event, Hugh Thomas. (One of the strengths of Badminton, enormous as it has now become as a sporting institution, is that there are continual links back to its heritage.)

The competition that year was a fascinating dual between the acknowledged top combination of Weldon and Kilbarry against the new girl on the scene, Sheila Willcox with her Windsor mount High and Mighty. Sheila went into the lead in the dressage only to be eclipsed by Weldon by 1.56 points. That gap never changed and Kilbarry took the title for the second year running. Sheila Willcox had however posted her credentials and there was much more to come.

In the early years just under 60 per cent of riders completed the event. This moved up to 65 per cent for a couple of years, but in 1956, supposedly over a tough pre-Olympic track, nearly 75 per cent made it. To cater for the increasing crowds the general layout changed. The start and finish were moved to an area somewhere between the current grandstand and The Lake, which had at one time been the final fence. The steeplechase moved from Didmarton to the Slaits adjacent to the airstrip.

The Willcox years

Kilbarry was killed in a first fence fall at the Cottesbrooke One Day Event in the spring of 1957, which made Sheila Willcox and High and Mighty the undisputed favourites for Badminton that year. They started as they meant to continue, giving a superb display in the dressage to score a remarkable 24.33. Dressage specialist Diana Mason with Tramella was close with 28.33 but was eliminated on the cross country. Sheila and High and Mighty, drawn last in each phase, never put a foot wrong, going fast and clear cross country and faultless in the show jumping to win by a margin of 25.79 from Penny Moreton for Ireland. Penny had a last minute ride on Red Sea. In the early 1950s Penny, born in Britain, had based herself at Lt. Colonel Hume Dudgeon's yard. The Colonel, whose son Ian had been runner up at the first Badminton, used to let her compete on 'spare' rides. In third place was the sporting Ted Marsh and Wild Venture.

In its early days the rules of eventing only allowed Army officers to compete. They then relented to include other ranks. Next, women were allowed in national competitions, then championships and finally in 1964 the Olympics. It was slow progress for the lady riders considering in 1957 there were five of them in the first eight places at Badminton. Also in 23rd place was David Somerset, who had taken over the ride on Countryman III from Bertie Hill, having bought him from the Queen, and the syndicate of among others, the Duke of Beaufort from whom he would inherit the title in 1984.

There were a then record 58 starters at the next Badminton, though the completion statistics dropped to 55 per cent again. Sheila Willcox had won the 1957 European Championships at Copenhagen and the big autumn event at Harewood in 1956. Her dressage score with High and Mighty at 37.00 was 22.67 points ahead of their nearest rival, Ted Marsh and Wild Venture. To put this in context the worst score was 170.00 for the unfortunate Beatrice Elizabeth Shaw and Double Diamond who, perhaps unsurprisingly, failed to complete.

For the second year running Sheila could not be caught from day one and finished with a plus score of 68.20. Runner up was Major Derek Allhusen with Laurien 47 points adrift. Allhusen had also had his appetite for this 'new' sport whetted at the 1948 Olympics. The combination had won team gold at the previous year's Copenhagen Europeans.

Over the years a pattern emerged. Some of the older names seemed to stay competing at Badminton for a long time. John Oram was fourth in 1958. In third place was Anneli Drummond-Hay riding Pluto. Some of the horses stayed around too. Countryman III moved up the order to seventh with David Somerset.

Badminton 1959 saw a radical, and not necessarily popular innovation. Over 100 entries had been received, even after more stringent qualification rules had been recently introduced. The previous year the

dressage judges had had to sit through 58 tests. Today it is accepted that any more than 40 per day is excessive. With the prospect of a massive starting line up, an extra day of dressage was mooted. Neither the Duke nor the organising committee were keen on this, so the decision was made to split the entry in two, with two judging panels working concurrently. The section for the more qualified horses would be called The Great Badminton Championship Event (senior) and the other The Little Badminton Event (junior). All the phases of the competition would be identical. The unconvincing spin at the time was that the sections were named after the two villages of the titles. The pejorative 'Little' hardly helped the esteem of section B. Ironically, when the competitors came to post there were only 24 in the top section and 27 in the other. Throughout the six years of the split competition the highest combined number of starters was 59, only one more than the marathon of 1958, and the lowest 35, with 19 in one section and 16 in the other respectively.

Sheila was now Mrs Waddington and came with Airs and Graces and promptly took the 'Great' section to become the only person to have won the event three years running. In second place was the evergreen Countryman III and David Somerset and Ted Marsh was third again with the consistent Wild Venture.

Winner of the 'Little' section was the previous year's dressage wooden spoon, Double Diamond, still not great at that phase but under Shelagh Kesler rose to the occasion on the cross country.

The weather was atrocious throughout the event and it was very nearly cancelled. The course was inspected on the Friday night and it was decided to continue, but with a modified course. Five fences were removed altogether and four more were altered. The park was left in a dreadful state, but at the prize giving the Duke announced that he was looking forward to welcoming everybody back the following year.

The wizards from Oz

The Australians had come over en masse in 1956 and, with another Olympics on the horizon at Rome in the summer of 1960, decided to use Badminton as their prep competition again. Flying horses from Australia to Europe in those days was too much of a risk, so the squad came over by ship. They had to leave six months before the Olympics and the boat trip lasted five weeks. They had to go via Italy to offload wool en route. To keep the horses in work they laid a school on the deck and rode most days. Pipe opening fast work was out of the question!

In the early days horses arrived at Badminton by several methods. Some even arrived by train at the now defunct Badminton railway station.

Because of the devastation to the ground from the previous year the dressage and jumping were removed from in front of the house, never to return. In the early days, with small crowds the house provided a superb backdrop, but with the need for grandstands the new venue, further into the park, suited the purpose perfectly.

The weather was fine throughout the event and the Australians were in cracking form. Heading the pack was a wiry New South Wales dairy farmer Bill Roycroft (whose autograph I have just found in a copy of Barbara Cooper's book I am using for research). He was riding the 15hh ex-polo pony Our Solo. Second was Laurie Morgan with Salad Days. Both the Australians moved up on the final day when the overnight leader Anneli Drummond-Hay faulted twice in the show jumping to finish third. Fourth for Australia was Neale John Lavis with Morrabooka, John Kelly was 10th riding Adlai, and Brian Crago came 11th on Toscanello.

There had been another spectator incident when a child ran out in front of Capt. Norman Arthur and Blue Jeans. The child was bowled over, unhurt, but Arthur sportingly pulled up to see if the child was all right, losing valuable time. He finished fifth.

For the Australians all the work paid off, as they also won gold in Rome.

The Australians were certainly getting the hang of Badminton, and Laurie Morgan, who had earlier done well with Gold Ross and had been runner up the previous year with Salad Days, came back to see if they could go one better. Just to emphasise the versatility of these riders, Laurie had decided to take in some nonchalant steeplechasing on his 1961 visit. He proceeded to win the Foxhunters at the Cheltenham Festival with College Master and then took on the Grand National course and won that Foxhunters as well. His Badminton campaign nearly came unstuck when he discovered he had learned the wrong dressage test. He just about got it right but lost a few points for errors of course, which might have proved expensive.

It had been very wet before the event but on dressage day there had at least been a drying wind. Unfortunately it rained again on cross country day, making the going very sticky, or as *The Times* wrote 'like soft toffee'. There were 27 starters in the senior section, of which only 15 finished the event. To give some indication of the action during the afternoon, Mike Bullen slipped and fell at the Irish Bank with Sea Breeze and Cottage Romance gave him a ducking at the Open Water. They duly finished fourth and third respectively! Lying in second place after the cross country was Harry Freeman-Jackson and St Finbarr for Ireland. They show jumped clear, putting the pressure on Morgan, who by now might rue those dressage errors. He nursed Salad Days round the track so cautiously that despite clearing every fence they received .75 time penalties. But it was enough and Australia won Badminton for the second year in a row.

The original purpose of Badminton as a training ground for the British team had been completely superseded. In a dozen events there had been British, Irish, Swiss and Australian winners. Badminton had become the unofficial annual World Championships: the event everybody wanted to win.

A good friend of the 10th Duke was Colonel Bill Whitbread, of the brewing dynasty. Out hunting with Beaufort one day he suggested that his company would like to 'support' the event. He didn't suggest anything too overt, understanding that the event was Badminton's and the Duke's, but he would like to present a trophy and contribute to the prize fund. Whitbread had become the first commercial sponsor of horse racing with the Whitbread Gold Cup at Sandown. Under this low-key approach Whitbread's name didn't initially show on the programme. Then modestly it stated 'Badminton Horse Trials for the Whitbread Trophy' and eventually, when a bit more commercialisation was deemed appropriate, 'The Whitbread Championships Badminton'. The Whitbread sponsorship was one of the longest ever in sport, spanning 31 years, 1961–1991 inclusive. The handsome Garrard trophy, depicting a top hat and tailed rider astride a thoroughbred 'at ease' became one of sports most recognisable prizes. Smaller replicas were minted each year for presentation to the top 12 riders, and ownership of one of these was a real status symbol. (While researching my first book, *Horse Laughs*, in 1982, I was asked to lunch by HRH Princess Anne and Mark Phillips at Gatcombe Park. On the sideboard in their dining room there was what could only be described as a regiment of these, won by the two of them in preceding years, and rather impressive it looked too.)

On film

The big autumn Three Day Event at Harewood had been replaced in 1961 by a new event at Burghley. The winner of that first Burghley was Anneli Drummond-Hay, who had been third at Badminton in 1960 on Perhaps. Her new star ride was Merely a Monarch. At Badminton in 1962 Anneli started the competition with a dressage score which was

over 30 points ahead of her nearest rival, Susan Fleet and The Gladiator.

Only three riders managed maximum bonus that year: Anneli, Frank Weldon with Young Pretender, and the always thrusting Mike Bullen on Sea Breeze. They filled the top three spots, but Anneli's winning margin was a whopping 42 points.

Taking a providence-tempting punt, Whitbread decided to make a documentary about Anneli's build up to Badminton, following all her preparations, arrival at the event and the competition. Murphy's Law dictates that these ventures always go pear shaped, and just as appearing on the preview cover of *Horse & Hound* before the big event spells disaster, so usually would a documentary. However, the gods were with Whitbread, and the subsequent film can be more than partially blamed for firing your author's ambition to ride at Badminton.

PART 2

AMBITION IGNITED (1963–1974)

An epiphany

Although my father had shown a passing interest in horses during his Army career, having ridden in a couple of flat races in India and being secretary of the Quetta Hunt in what is now Pakistan, we were not even remotely a 'horsey' family. My parents had spectated at Badminton in 1952, the year Mark Darley won on Emily Little, before I was born, and I have vague memories of being taken one year as a child. Badminton certainly didn't register as anything other than an outing.

In 1962 I was at day school in Camberley, Surrey, oddly only about a mile away from the site of the 1948 Olympics, and one of my best friends at the time was a chap called David Willett. He was the son of the *Horse & Hound* racehorse breeding expert Peter Willett, and he was having riding lessons. Out of the blue my father asked if I would like to have a go, and so it was that on New Year's day in the freezing winter of 1963, at Cross Lanes Riding School, Arborfield, I was plonked on to Miss Muffet and spent an hour circling on the lunge under the tutelage of a certain Lockie Richards. It all seemed rather fun, and inevitably, to ensure the next lesson was booked, my 'seat' was complimented. Sensibly, no expensive riding gear had been bought. Apart from a proper hat, I wore cord trousers with elastic sewn to go under my brown walking shoes.

My poor mother, who never was, and never will be horsey (Hoorah), nearly froze to death that winter sitting in the gallery, as her little darling was going round and round and round.

It must have been decided by my eighth birthday in 1963 that I was genuinely keen, because as a complete surprise a pony was produced. Nothing in my subsequent equestrian life quite went right first time, and I discovered that the procurement of my pony had been somewhat drama filled.

A local character, Smith, a rag and bone man, had been put on the case and found an apparently ideal pony. Sadly, just before my birthday it got out on the road, was hit and had to be put down. (I only heard about this years later.) It's probably best not to speculate, but Smith found another one in the nick of time and I became the proud owner of Noddy, a four-year-old New Forrest/Dartmoor cross, standing at 12.2hh.

To say we were ignorant would be an understatement, but by literally doing it by the book, the still excellent Pony Club Manual, we muddled along nicely. Those first ponies are make or break when it comes to keeping up the interest level of an eight-year-old. Noddy turned out to be a star, and by the end of the year we had joined the local Staff College and Sandhurst Pony Club.

At one unmounted rally we were all ushered into a tack room for a lecture on how to assemble a bridle and then sat on the floor as a film screen was brought out . . . 'Whitbread presents . . . '

If 1963 was my epiphany, Badminton itself was having to cope with one of the worst winters on record. The early freeze turned to rain in the spring. It seemed at one point that the event might have to be cancelled. For several years the park had been completely trashed, and it was very generous of the Duke to let this happen on what seemed to be a yearly basis. Of course the equestrian part of the competition didn't do much damage, but Badminton was now a very popular spectator event with large crowds and lots of cars. That aside, the organisers, as ever, considered the welfare of the horses as paramount.

It was decided that the competition would go ahead, but in One Day Event format, which meant no endurance phases of roads and tracks and steeplechase, and the show jumping preceding the cross country.

There were only 13 starters in the senior section with seven of those failing to get round. Susan Fleet and The Gladiator again did a good dressage test, and beat Richard Meade on Barberry by just over 23 points.

Ironically the junior section (Little Badminton) had more runners (15) and only three failed to get round. This section was won by Sgt. Ben Jones on Master Bernard.

With only 18 completions, for once the crowd might have felt themselves a bit short changed, but by now Badminton had become an institution and the general feeling was of looking forward to normal service being resumed.

As the sport progressed it seemed to move further and further away from its military roots. There were indeed several competitors each year from the Services, but they had been joined by farmers, hunting ladies and an occasional aristocrat. The organisational backbone of the sport though, was to remain militarily influenced for many more years. When I wrote *Horse Laughs* in 1982 the main committee and staff of the British Horse Society, which then oversaw Horse Trials, included no fewer than two Generals, 13 Colonels and 13 Majors.

Capt. James Templer had been British cross-country skiing champion before deciding to take up eventing seriously. With his horse M'Lord Connelly he had become individual European Champion at Burghley in 1962 and had a win at Badminton very much in his sights for 1963. He was very disappointed when the event was contracted to a One Day Event, and didn't run that year. His preparation for Badminton 1964 was unusual, as he decided the best approach would be to go to the event fresh, without a single competitive run beforehand. To conserve his horse's energy he also ran alongside it for the entire roads and tracks, which would have been considerably over 10 miles (16km), in riding boots. Well it all worked, as he won with a 27-point lead over another soldier, Jeremy Smith-Bingham and By Golly.

Little Badminton that year saw yet another win for Sheila (Willcox) Waddington riding Glenamoy, making her at that stage Badminton's most successful competitor. 1964 also saw the end of what could be termed the first phase in the development of Badminton. Colonel Gordon Cox-Cox retired and with him 'Babe' Moseley, who had also been assistant to the first director, Trevor Horn. David Somerset took over as director and appointed Frank Weldon as course designer. Spurning the received idea of relaxing the course after an Olympic year, Weldon started as he meant to go on, and frightened everybody by racking the whole thing up a notch.

Family outings

As a family we had started going to Badminton now with much more interest. I had begun jumping some makeshift obstacles in Noddy's paddock and was now really taking an interest in the heroics of the Badminton riders as they aimed themselves at what seemed impossible challenges. We would specially go to watch feature fences like The Quarry, and right at the farthest end of the course, the massive Vicarage Ditch, basically just a brush with a ditch in front but vast from the viewpoint of a 4ft (1.22m) nine-year-old. This obstacle never let the crowd down as it usually unseated somebody. There were even then the occasional 'technical' fences such as the Cat's Cradle, a fiendish arrangement of angled poles.

We only ever used to go on the Saturday, considering those who went to watch the dressage far too keen, and we always watched the show jumping on telly the next day. The Saturday routine, however, we got down to a fine art. Much has been done over the years to ease the traffic into the park on cross-country day, but there will always be queues, so it is best to accept it and leave enough time to get there for lunch. We always took a picnic which we had probably raided while in the traffic. We would then set off round the course, sometimes last fence first, and see at least one combination over each one. In those days you could go right up to the fences between horses and I would fantasise 'one day' . . .

The big story of 1965, despite the popular win of Ireland's Eddie Boylan, who had been 10th at the very first Badminton, and Duras Eile, was the remarkable feat of Bill Roycroft. He came second in the senior section with Eldorado and sixth with Stoney Crossing, who by way of preparation had run third in the Cheltenham Gold Cup behind Arkle and Mill House, and he was also runner up in the Little Badminton section with Avatar. Bill would have covered well over 40 miles (64km) of competitive track. Little Badminton that year was won by Martin Whiteley on his own The Poacher, a horse that would become a mainstay of the British team.

In 1966 I started having riding lessons at Tweseldown with the 'local' Badminton rider Celia Ross-Taylor. She put me on a schoolmaster pony of hers and I started to learn the intricacies of 'shoulder in' and 'on the bit'. That year I went with Noddy to my first ever Pony Club event at Englefield Park near Reading, managed to remember my dressage test and got a rosette. I was taken there, without family, by Pat Sutton, a former Pony Club Champion (who also gave me some lessons) because there had been a mild domestic at home. Some long lost relatives of my father from Jamaica were coming to lunch, and my mother had expected me to be present! By another coincidence, for the last 30 years my parents have lived on the edge of the Englefield Estate.

It was another appalling year for weather, but ever optimistic, all arrangements were made at Badminton. Riders had started to arrive the day before their briefing and everyone kept their fingers crossed. This time, however, there really was no alternative but to cancel. Bitterly disappointing for all concerned, but in true style the traditional cocktail party at Badminton House took place anyway.

Mr Somerset handed over the director's reins to Frank Weldon and took the role of chairman of the event. Frank was determined to make Badminton a commercial success, to which end he binned some of the periphery show classes and also the Little Badminton concept. Badminton was to be Badminton and that was that. He also instigated the continuing practice of having the show-jumping phase run in reverse order of placing to create maximum tension. His cross-country courses always had the knack of terrifying the riders, but most jumped very well.

The 1967 course was the one abandoned the previous year.

Duras Eile led the dressage, but excitingly for me, my trainer Celia Ross-Taylor was in third place with Jonathan. They remained there after the cross country. Going third last in the show jumping, they went clear. Next to go was Derek Allhusen with Lochinvar, who kicked down five to drop to 11th. Last to go was the 1965 winner, Eddie Boylan, who had been in the lead since the dressage. He had two down and my trainer had won Badminton!

The galloping nurse

On arrival at the event on cross country day as a spectator, I was always dispatched to buy a couple of programmes. We would then go through the list of entries to see if there were any 'locals' to support. Celia wasn't there to defend her title in 1968, but there was Eric Thompson, a Badminton stalwart, whose twin brother Boris had taught me at Pony Club Camp and Tom Durston-Smith, who was in the Hawley Riding Club with my father. The 'galloping nurse' Jane Bullen, Mike's younger sister, had been fifth the previous year on the diminutive Our Nobby and had been flagged up by the press. The horse's name was sufficiently similar to my pony Noddy, by then in full swing with my sister Katie, that they deserved a cheer. In his Army past my father had instructed at the Royal Military Academy Sandhurst, so was intrigued to see an Officer Cadet entered. He suggested we also follow the fortunes of this young Mark Phillips fellow.

The leader after the dressage was the popular Sgt Ben Jones with Foxdor, with Michael Plumb for the USA second and Ireland's Juliet Jobling-Purser third with Jenny.

Add the two facts that Frank Weldon was getting into his stride as course designer and it was an Olympic year, the cross-country course was the biggest anyone had ever seen at Badminton. The 12th fence, a wide ditch with a post and rail away, eliminated 14 of the first 15 horses to start. The only exception was Lorna Sutherland. This carnage would be unacceptable today, not least because it would deprive the spectators further on in the course any action for about an hour! As it happened, only 24 of the original 55 starters completed the event. Richard Meade and Turnstone could only manage 18th after the dressage and Our Nobby was equally off the pace in 23rd, however both put in superb cross-country rounds and climbed right up the leader board. Ben Jones, though slower on Foxdor, kept his place courtesy of his superior dressage.

Meade and Bullen show jumped clear, putting pressure on the last to go. Sadly Foxdor rolled the second fence and it was all over. Bullen the 'galloping nurse' had won and Richard Meade was second. Jones slipped to third and in fourth place was that young Officer Cadet with Rock On. It was a good year for the British as they took the top eight places, with Major Derek Allhusen fifth on Lochinvar.

Probably for the first time since the first Badminton, 1968 was a genuine pointer to the forthcoming Mexico Olympics. All of the top five placed were in our Olympic squad. Phillips was reserve, Jane Bullen went with Our Nobby, Ben Jones went with The Poacher and Richard Meade was gifted the ride on Mary Gordon-Watson's Cornishman V. The team won gold and Derek Allhusen took individual silver with Lochinvar.

I went to Harrow in the autumn of 1968, aged 13, where the whole school had to take part in something called the Churchill Essay Prize. Every boy had to write no fewer than a thousand words on any topic. A thousand seemed an awful lot in those days, but I decided I would write about the exploits of our victorious Mexico team, and the almost impossible flood conditions on the cross-country course. Not exactly Pulitzer Prize winning stuff, but it was my first go at writing about a sport I was really beginning to take an interest in, and that made finding the thousand words much easier.

By now I had a super speedy pony called Zombie and was a member of my Pony Club eventing team. The dream of riding at Badminton was not perhaps looking so outrageous. Always wanting to look the part, we had bought a crash helmet and silk from the Herbert Johnson stand at Badminton. 'I'll wear this hat here one day' I promised myself. In those days it was considered rather posy to wear grown-up cross-country gear, but as I was still on ponies I still wore short joddy boots. Long boots were for riding horses.

We pulled into the car park at Badminton in 1969, and as usual I was sent off to get some programmes. When I got back to the car, who should pull up and park behind us as a paying punter but last year's winner Jane Bullen? Programme in hand, I got her autograph.

There was another strong field of 48 riders, mainly British but with two Roycroft entries and James Scanlon from Australia and Caroline Lockhart and Denise Johnson from Ireland. The favourites were to fall like flies. Ben Jones and The Poacher retired after the dressage, Bertie Hill fell on the steeplechase with Chicago having led the dressage phase, Sheila Willcox crushed her ribs when Fair and Square broke down in Huntsman's Close and fell and Richard Meade retired Barberry after a ducking in The Lake, loosing his bridle.

A fall would give you 60 penalties and put you out of the running.

In 1967 Colonel 'Babe' Moseley had instigated the Junior European Championships, held the first year at Eridge in Sussex. Only the French came to challenge Great Britain at that event. The individual winner was Richard Walker with the Anglo-Arab Pasha. The following year, when the Championships had got going properly and were held in France, the combination won it again. The Walkers had tried to sell Pasha in the spring of 1969 but there were no takers, so they decided to enter for Badminton. There was some interest in Richard that year because of his junior record, and also, at 18, he was of the youngest age eligible to compete. With the established stars all over the place, Richard found himself in the lead after the cross country. A clear round in the show jumping from Angela Martin-Bird moved her up to second, Roycroft's two mounts Warrathoola and Furtive had secured third and fourth, but a safe clear round by Pasha gave Walker the kudos of being the youngest ever winner of Badminton.

First steps

Though I was proud to have had lessons with a future Badminton winner (Celia Ross-Taylor) some years back, I was rather jealous of my Pony Club girlfriend, Terry Clarke, whose family seemed to know famous rider Lorna Sutherland well enough to get Christmas cards from her. This was eased slightly when Lorna stabled her famous coloured horse Popadom with us before the Liphook Horse Trials, one of the warm-up competitions for Badminton. Although Lorna lived in Scotland it also transpired she was a great friend of Celia. These people who had been distant stars to me were very slowly entering an orbit of at least acquaintance. Indeed while in the car queue in Badminton village for the 1970 event, Tom Durston-Smith, in all his riding gear, stopped to say hello. I'm sure that impressed the people in the car behind!

Despite the Estate's objection to running two days of dressage in 1959, the number of entries was now such that in 1970 it was adopted.

Weldon excelled himself with 'rider frightener' fences in the cross country that year, introducing his version of the Normandy Bank, which he had seen at the European Championships at Haras du Pin, France. It goes without saying that Weldon's version was much bigger than the original. Basically you were meant to jump up a bank on to a plateau and take off immediately over a post and rail then fly through space over an enormous drop. It was one of Frank's genius fences. It looked absolutely fantastic in photographs, impressed the spectators no end, but was in fact a remarkably jumpable fence. For many years it was *the* iconic Badminton obstacle. (Later in the 1970s a friend of mine, Fraser Jack, was very philosophical about failing to complete the course two years running. He claimed to have been round the whole course, albeit over two years. 'I got as far as the Normandy Bank going one way round and got as far as the same fence going the other way the next time.') Following the Normandy Bank was another much talked about fence, The Ski Jump, a log on to a very steep ramp then up a hill to a spread fence. Over the years there were several variations to this.

The Poacher was now effectively owned by the British team. Richard Meade was nominally the British team captain, and as the joke went at the time: 'Richard has his jackets, boots and horses made for him.' He got the ride. The Poacher led from the front and Meade won with less than a fence to spare from Ireland's Ronnie MacMahon and San Carlos. But disaster befell Bertie Hill and Chicago, who were sure of a top place until they show jumped fence ten instead of six, and were promptly eliminated.

The main talking point of the year however was Lorna Sutherland emulating Bill Roycroft's achievement of five years earlier, and completing with three horses. It had never really been her intention to take three. Popadom was her own but Gypsy Flame and The Dark Horse were owned by others, and the owners were keen for a run. Lorna took the practical view that by the law of averages one would drop out before the event, but none did. She was committed. Gypsy Flame came fourth, Popadom was 12th and the Dark Horse came 15th. Lorna had jumped 132 fences and covered 48 miles (77km). She also did this without the help of a professional groom, doing all the plaiting etc. herself.

The scoring system was changed in 1971, as it did many times over the years, now based purely on penalties. No longer could riders gain plus points on the cross country. There were 48 starters that year, with five from Ireland and one each from Switzerland and Sweden.

The Queen and other members of the Royal Family had been regular visitors since the 1950s, however this year Princess Anne made

her first appearance on the home bred Doublet. This development, of course, thrust Badminton on to the front pages of the papers. The Princess had been encouraged into eventing by Colonel Sir John Miller and was trained near Windsor by Alison Oliver.

Despite being hassled by photographers while warming up for her dressage, who ignored her treatise to 'Naff off', the Princess and Doublet lay second after the dressage to Mark Phillips and Great Ovation. She clocked up 32 unnecessary time penalties on the steeplechase but went clear cross country and had just one show jump down to finish a very creditable fifth, earning the first of her replica silver horses. Mark Phillips and Great Ovation won by a 30-point margin from Mary Gordon-Watson, third the previous year, having managed to wrestle the ride on Cornishman V back from the British team captain. Honour was satisfied as Mary went on to become both European and World individual Champion and a team gold medallist the following year at the Munich Olympics. Another favourite of the era, Debbie West came third with Baccarat and Richard Walker was fourth on his new ride Upper Strata. Lined up in sixth and seventh were Mike Tucker, now the TV voice of eventing, and Angela Sowden, who was to become Mrs Mike Tucker.

In the spring of 1972, my A-level year, I had somehow managed to sufficiently impress 'Babe' Moseley, chairman of the junior selectors and his committee, at a regional trial, to be put on the shortlist for the Junior European Championships. I was back under the auspices of Celia Ross-Taylor, who had found and prepared for me a steel grey thoroughbred whom I named the Purple People Eater (a 1960s song since you ask.)

In those days there were only three Three Day Events in Britain, in ascending order of difficulty: Tidworth, Burghley and Badminton. Tidworth was the venue for the team trial and the event was in May. My A levels were in June. It took a bit of persuading to get my Housemaster to give me the week off. To put in some riding practice I would cycle from Harrow to Suzanne's riding establishment and ride one of the school horses under the eye of showman Richard Ramsay. This was probably not the best preparation for my first Three Day Event, despite Richard's best efforts. Perhaps unsurprisingly we failed to get round, but the experience of doing roads and tracks and steeplechase, coupled with the thrill of even being considered in international terms was fantastic.

Badminton 1972 is remembered mostly for the memory of Richard Meade, last to go in the show jumping with Laurieston, being so cautious that he accumulated 1.25 time penalties and gifted the Whitbread trophy to Mark Phillips who won with Great Ovation for the second year running.

However, a contemporary of mine, Brynley Powell, from my old Pony Club, was entered on Breakaway, so riding at Badminton seemed possible. As it happened, Bryn retired on the cross country, but he had been there. Bryn now runs Tweseldown Racecourse.

I was still quite young, and completed my last A level on my 17th birthday. The deal was that if I passed them all I could leave school and have a gap year, concentrating on the horses before going off to Saint Martins School of Art the following September. I think I scraped my French by about 1 per cent.

I'd enjoyed the steeplechase so much that I decided to retire Purple People Eater from his slightly reluctant eventing career and decided to take him point to pointing. I now had two mares, Cabaret, whom we had bought from Sally Davis, another member of the Pony Club team. (We had joined forces with the Clapham family and almost had a private little Pony Club with the Garth South.) The other mare was a little Arab called Samena. That autumn I went round the circuit with Celia having some modest success, but getting a great deal of experience.

In the spring of 1973 Celia suggested that I should go and have some residential training at a competition yard. There were three main centres then, which all the serious contenders would go to. In the west country Bertie Hill had the likes of Mark Phillips. At Bracknell Alison Oliver had Princess Anne and others, and at Waterstock near Oxford, Swedish trainer Lars Sederholm had Richard Walker as head trainer and riders such as the sporting amateur and former jump jockey Chris Collins, who used to helicopter in for lessons. Cabaret and I were sent to Lars.

I had been shortlisted for the juniors again, this time with Cabaret. That was my spring target, but the yard had at least half a dozen horses and riders preparing for Badminton. I was now really amongst it, and despite the shock of actually having to 'do' my own horse, it was absolute magic. Not least I was actually being taught by my hero, Richard Walker. It was at Waterstock that I met one of my now best friends, Alex Colquhoun, who had made the junior team the year before with Belle Grey. Here was a good mate who was going for the big one and became Chairman of the Young Riders selectors from 2009.

Badminton that year had the largest field to date of 69 starters. It was always jokingly said that Frank Weldon never made mistakes. Maybe it was deliberate then that 23 were eliminated on the cross country, mostly at the third fence, the Coffin, nine retired and six pulled out after the roads and tracks. Only 30 completed the event.

Improving on her impressive fifth place debut the previous year, Lucinda Prior-Palmer, the granddaughter of a Viceroy of India, had her name engraved on the famous trophy. Richard Meade was runner up again, this time on Bar Hammond's Eagle Rock and my friend Alex got round to finish in 23rd place, one above Hugh Thomas and Playamar. The other memorable feat of 1973 was when Rachel Bayliss and her horse Gurgle the Greek slithered into the Stockholm Fence, a deep ditch with a tree trunk over it, went under the trunk and emerged unpenalised the other side. They had been between the regulation red and white flags, so no penalties. Modern fence construction tends to make this no longer possible.

My Tidworth was more successful than the previous year insofar as I completed my first Three Day Event. I never did make the junior team, but I was now a genuine Three Day Eventer. The preparations for my first Burghley that September were almost as ludicrously casual as that for my first Tidworth, as I had inadvertently got myself selected to go on a Pony Club international exchange to Japan for the whole of August. There didn't seem to be much riding at the selection day, but quite a lot of socialising at the bar at British Horse Society HQ, by then based at Stoneleigh, Warwickshire. I was on the team!

Once again Celia did all the prep work with Cabaret and I literally got off the plane from Tokyo and went straight to Burghley. I very nearly got round. Again the thrill was immense because there were real crowds, TV cameras, the works. There was one small problem, however, I needed another Three Day Event under my belt to qualify for Badminton 1974.

I had started at art school the week after Burghley, but had to take some time out that first term to go to the Wylye event at Lord and Lady Hugh Russell's farm and eventing centre in Wiltshire. We had just taken delivery of our eventing caravan and emerging from that into pouring rain on Salisbury Plain, we went clear and had qualified. One of the first to congratulate me was 'Babe' Moseley.

After the event Cabaret was turned out for a holiday and I recall saying to her as I took off her head collar, 'when you next come in for work, guess where we are going'.

Shattered dreams

During all those years of spectating, and standing by a jump, programme in hand, waiting for the next rider to come, I always used to think to myself: 'I want my name in that programme one day.' In retrospect I should have raised my ambitions beyond that.

By 1974 I was now in my second term at Saint Martins and embracing the art school life with enormous enthusiasm. There we were, a bunch of supposedly talented 19-year-olds based in the Charing Cross Road, a stone's throw away from Soho, in the days before they had cleaned it up. It was a far cry from both Harrow and Waterstock. Luckily, however, it was my underlying equestrian ambition that kept me roughly on the narrow, if not entirely the straight!

Cabaret had come in and gone back to Celia and we set about the spring season, starting with the Advanced Crookham Two Day Event at good old Tweseldown. This was the first event of the season and all the top guns were there. Though I had been in senior competition for over a year, it was still a thrill to be in the collecting ring with Richard Meade, Princess Anne, Mark Phillips et al. The point of those old-fashioned Two Day Events was that they included a modest roads and tracks phase and a steeplechase, here around the very track they used at the 1948 Olympics. We went clear cross country and the build up was going to plan.

At the beginning of April the special envelope arrived. In it were the list of entries, the competitor's car pass and badge, some general instructions and an invitation to the cocktail party in Badminton House on the Thursday of the event.

It was not to be. Less than a week before the event Cabaret pulled up lame after a bit of fast work. Shattered dreams etc. etc. My college girlfriend, Annie Wild, couldn't see what all the fuss was about. She was a very good reality check, reminding me that there may be more to life than Badminton, especially if my loved one was completely underwhelmed by my ambition. . . 'Who am I kidding?' I blubbed.

With the benefit of hindsight it may have been a blessing in disguise. Though the course was arguably easier than it had been for several years, Badminton was probably an ambition too far for a super genuine Pony Club campaigner. Cabaret later became my sister's favourite hunter and we bred the Olympic gold medal winning horse Justin Thyme from her.

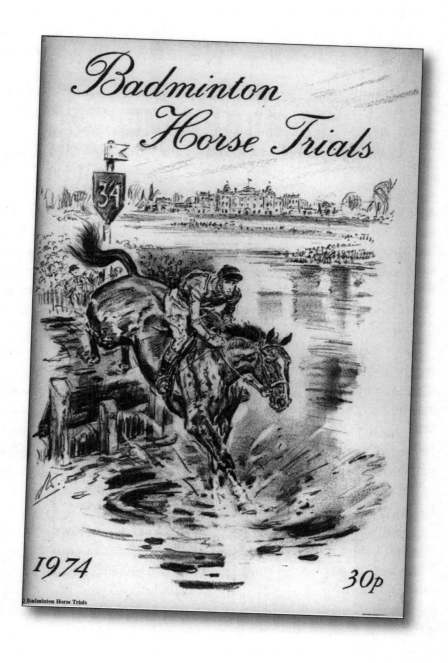

Anyway, I had my Badminton badges so I was going to go and have some fun. Now you will understand why my ambition for a name in the programme was not enough. I was in the programme all right, but that was it.

My art school sartorial 'sense' kicked in. At 19 I was a mere slip of a boy. My wardrobe for cross country day consisted of flared denim dungarees, no shirt, a short mink coat, Cuban heeled boots, a buttoned tweed cap, a clip-on gold earring and a hint of eye shadow. Oh yes, and my competitor's badge.

Somehow a group of us found ourselves in an 'access all areas' Land Rover with a 'Rover' pass and had a wonderful VIP day watching the competition from our raised vantage point around the course.

Princess Anne did the best dressage test with Doublet, but fell on the steeplechase and retired. Any fall on the 'chase' was really annoying as the phase was only meant as a time trial and a mental pipe opener for both horse and rider. You were not meant to have jumping faults on this phase, though someone always did.

A new fence, about a third of the way round the cross-country course, was an S-shaped post and rails on an incline, which was flagged to invite three jumping efforts. Last year's winners Lucinda Prior-Palmer and Be Fair, having already had a stop at The Quarry, fell there, as did John Kersley, the very talented second jockey to the Bertie Hill yard. Riding Classic Chips he had been 'miked up' by the BBC. The live coverage was unable to bleep him. Later in the day Matt Straker, one of the veterans of my Japanese Pony Club expedition, fell at the very last fence and also turned the air blue.

There was a controversial incident that year involving the future World Champion Bruce Davidson and Irish Cap for America. He had based himself in England since January for a concerted attempt on the title. He was to be a victim of his own professionalism. Put bluntly, there had been a cock up. The optimum time given to the competitors differed by 10 seconds to the one used by the official time keepers.

Bruce, being an almost obsessive perfectionist, timed his round to just squeak inside the time. A cynic might say he was trying to be too clever, because frankly 10 seconds in over 12 minutes is nothing, and a sensible rider could have given themselves a bit of a cushion. Anyway the upshot was he was given 13.6 time penalties. His appeal fell on deaf ears, on the slightly dubious grounds that it was the same for all the riders. Debbie Sly speculates in her book what Frank Weldon must have thought privately, as many years back he had lost the event through a timing error. Bruce came third, but the enduring myth that he would have won without those time penalties is wrong. It is here that I am indebted to Rhydain Wynn-Williams' statistics tome (Rhydain's Bible, as we call it).

The eventual winner was Mark Phillips on the Queen's Columbus, who finished on their dressage score of 40.33. Bruce's dressage was 41.67.

PART 3

THE COMPETITIVE YEARS (1975–1981)

A non-event

During the summer of 1974 I had Cabaret on the circuit again, and had qualified for the British Open finals, then held at Cirencester Park. Somehow she didn't feel right on the cross country, so I pulled up halfway round. While walking back to the horse lines I decided to retire her. I did however conjure up a cunning plan. Celia had the ride on two decent three day horses. One was called Nimrod, which she had ridden at Badminton in 1973 but had retired on the cross country, and another, an Anglo-Arab, by Question, called Master Question, which had completed the Dutch Three Day at Boekelo and been fifth in the senior section at Tidworth that year. Both horses belonged to outside owners.

It was no real secret that Celia wanted to retire from top level eventing, and was more interested in show jumping. There were two of us likely lads in the yard, myself and the currently successful dressage trainer Andrew Day. One way or another Andrew got the ride on Nimrod and completed a Three Day Event in Belgium. Master Question had been on the market, for a sum way out of our bracket, as his owner/breeder Pamela Gormley was beginning to baulk at the training fees. Back at the horsebox I outlined my hastily conceived plan to my father. 'I think we ought to retire Cabaret, but how about suggesting to Pamela that we pay the keep if I have the ride?' It was a bit cheeky and obviously I would need Celia's blessing and help. She backed the idea straight away, and I wrote to Pamela the following day. The deal was on.

The following spring was full of anticipation. I was a very lucky 19-year-old with the ride on a proper Three Day Event horse.

As a small sartorial diversion it is worth noting that not everyone, by any means, wore top hats and tails for the dressage at big events in those days. But with my smart new horse I thought it would be appropriate. A tailor-made tailcoat however cost a king's ransom. I had another

51

cunning plan. There are basically three shapes of tailcoat. The wedding gear morning coat curves down from the collar with a single button that can be done up or left open. The 'white tie' dress tailcoat has a cutaway shape below the collar with six double-breasted faux buttons and is worn open. The dressage coat is cutaway but fronted by six double-breasted buttons that do fasten.

I went to Moss Bros and bought one of their old 'for hire' dress tailcoats and took it to college. In my tailoring classes I converted it into a dressage coat, sewing some coins into the tails to ensure a good hang when riding. It saved me a fortune.

We had a good first outing at Crookham and also at the Liphook event. It was another one of those blustery rainy springs, but the entry for Badminton was in, and the magic envelope duly arrived. Pamela was as excited as us as she had also always dreamt of participating at Badminton. She was actually quite lucky that Master Question turned out to be a horse at all, as he was out of a 13.2hh mare. To that end his stable name was Freak.

The rain kept coming, but Andrew and I didn't mind. We were going to Badminton. I can remember sitting with him in the caravan in Celia's mother's garden that he called home, reading every page of Barbara Cooper's book to get ourselves revved up.

We got to the event and sorted our caravans in the small field in Badminton Village behind the permanent Trials office. It was very wet. On the Wednesday the riders' briefing was held as usual in the village hall and it was the first time I heard some of the famous Weldonisms:

'Just remember this event is for the paying customers, not you. You may walk round the park on a loose rein, but it's a jealous world so don't go too close to the fences.' Like the comedian Dave Allen, he had the top of one of his index fingers chopped, and he would jab the stump to make a point.

After the briefing we set off in the convoy round the roads and tracks, walked the steeplechase and came back for a caravan lunch. After that we went for our first look at the course. There was a jumble of timber called the Chevrons at about fence four, a double bounce with a very narrow head-on element. I honestly couldn't visualise my way through it. Never a good sign!

The rain kept coming, but undaunted we did the dressage. It was a bit of a farce as the arena got very cut up but it was easy to remember the test as you just followed the 'Winnie the Poo' tracks. Every time I dipped my head the guttering of the brim of my top hat drenched me.

By the end of Friday the whole park was a quagmire and the event was cancelled. There was to be another year to wait.

The remainder of the spring was a bit drier, and as a consolation we ran in the senior section at Tidworth. I rode the cross country in a storm, but managed to pip Celia's result of the previous year by coming fourth. At least then I felt I had justified being given the ride.

After Tidworth we turned Freak out for a break, only for him to put a foot through a gate. He went quite lame and we didn't really know if he would come back. We brought him home and I nursed him very slowly throughout the summer, taking it one step at a time. We entered Burghley more in hope than expectation.

Ever the one to have an unorthodox run up to a big event, I took him straight to Burghley without a run. He gave me the most fabulous school master ride, and to my astonishment we ended up 12th. Bring on Badminton 1976.

At last

The spring weather for the build up in 1976 was fine and there was no question that the event would run. One generous owner, Olive Jackson, had a fantastic set up at Frensham in Surrey, and used to invite a dozen or so local Badminton hopefuls to have a pre-season run through the Badminton dressage test in front of top trainer David Hunt.

We would then have a splendid lunch and sit down with our coffee to have our efforts talked through.

At last there was the chance genuinely to compete at Badminton. We arrived as ever on the Tuesday and settled in to the more intimate Portcullis Yard. It only stabled about six and we chose it every year. In the competitors' caravan park I was rather surprised to see my owner Pamela Gormley unload some hens which continued to cluck about the field for the rest of the event. I sometimes feel that much of my eventing career has taken place in some kind of parallel universe.

I was drawn to do dressage on the first day and put in quite a decent effort to lie sixth at that early stage. Indeed one of the three judges, Mike Bullen, had me top on the first day.

By the end of the second day I had dropped to a respectable 12th in the dressage. In Master Question I had a horse that on paper was in with a chance of a proper run.

The cross country course was the same as the one from the abandoned event of the previous year. That meant that the 'impossible' Chevrons at fence four were still there. Some riders, notably the Bertie Hill brigade, had anticipated that the fence would be there again and had built a replica at home. Little good would it do them as they all got penalties.

In those days riders would walk the course three times (probably more now). Riders have to work out their routes. The horses see it for the first time in competition. The first walk on the Wednesday was just to get a first impression, the second is when we would work out our routes in detail, and consider our Plan B's. Most of us went round with a trainer on the second walk. Although I was still with Celia, for many years I had had additional lessons with Dick Stillwell, who had coached several members of the British team. If it seems that I had a legion of trainers, it was because I needed all the help I could get. Dick was splendidly no-nonsense, and had just the type of positive approach to quell the nerves. During the walk round we always had to take account of the fact that any landmark we might consider as an aiming aid might be obscured by the crowd on the Saturday. The final walk was a no-doubts, no-hesitation affirmation of the route we intended to take. I was never tempted to do a Bruce Davidson and measure my way round. At this stage just getting round would be fine and I would go as fast as felt comfortable, not by the watch.

My father and I had developed a very workable sleeping arrangement, especially as we both snore. From Tuesday to Friday he would stay up the road at the Petty France Hotel and I would be in the caravan, but the night before the cross country I would have the posh room. For many years I would go to a dinner party with the Darling family at Hullavington, where Martin Whiteley always stayed. Caroline Darling had completed Badminton in 1974 and was probably one of the first of the second generation to compete at the event. Her late father rode in 1957. It was always a great way to take my mind off thoughts of Saturday.

Back in the hotel room and the course just went round and round my mind till I conked out.

The Starter for phase A of the roads and tracks was the friendly Tony Watson, who many years before had been one of my Pony Club District Commissioners. He doffed his bowler hat, wished me luck, and off I set on the speed and endurance phase. Phase A took us back past my hotel and on to the steeplechase course. I had ridden in half a dozen point to points by now, so probably had a small advantage over the majority who had only ever evented.

We were up on time as we approached the penultimate fence, completely missed our stride, and joined the ranks of 'there's always one' who wiped out on the steeplechase. There was grass sticking out of Freak's ear, skid marks on his backside and the telltale green stripe on my breeches. My strange memory, as I was reorganising myself, was the sight of a bearded and mounted Prince Charles witnessing my embarrassment with the Crown Equerry, Sir John Miller, Badminton veteran.

We got ourselves back together and set off on phase C. In the days of a long endurance phase we rode to Worcester Lodge, a folly at the end of the undulating Worcester Avenue, reputedly built to house an 18th century Duke's mistress. Looking a direct mile down the Avenue you can see Badminton House. My friend Alex Colquhoun had told me how exhilarating this final phase of the roads and tracks had been. Down in a dip you lost the House then saw it again as you rose to the top of an incline. As you got nearer you started to hear the loudspeaker commentary. Eventually you came to a large deer gate by The Ski Jump and a liveried Hunt Servant would let you into the park, and escort you through the crowds to the 10 minute rest pen.

Just beyond Worcester Lodge I spotted a single magpie. Was this a bad omen? A bit further on I realised that Freak wasn't trotting sound. Third time not lucky! I got off, and in the privacy of my isolation, let out a string of loud expletives and started the long walk home. I would put up a show of resigned composure back at base.

Every four minutes following riders would trot past offering their condolences. Eventually I got to the deer gate and was let into the park. A child proffering an autograph book approached. I managed a wry smile. I may not yet have jumped a cross country fence, but at least someone wants to know. 'Are you a rider?' she asked. I would have thought that my clothing and the horse on the end of the reins might have been a giveaway but whatever. 'Oh good. Could you please get me Lucinda's autograph?' 'No you little cherub I CAN'T. . . .'

In 1973 I had been the first of my gang to go to Burghley and the first to be placed in 1975, but in 1976 Brynley Powell, Tiny Clapham from my Pony Club Team and my best school friend, and subsequent Best Man, Adrian Ffooks all beat me in getting round Badminton – the only one I really wanted to crack. The really galling thing about failing at an annual ambition is that there is a whole year to wait before you get the chance to have another go. I did feel pretty low, but at least I never had to work out how to jump the Chevrons.

At the grown-up end of the competition three of the best known riders were on new mounts. Richard Meade was on Jacob Jones, Mark Phillips was there with Favour and Lucinda was riding Wideawake, a horse that had taken her some time to produce a rapport with. It turned out that the secret was to do as little as possible on board. Lucinda had won the Dutch event at Boekelo on the horse in the autumn and put in a polished performance at Badminton to take her second Whitbread Trophy. Phillips and Meade were third and fourth, but in second place was Hugh Thomas and Playamar. The main press picture on the Sunday, however, was of Mark Phillips lying on his back emptying the water from his boots after a ducking in The Lake from his second horse Brazil.

After the prize-giving the other placed riders were leaving the arena. Lucinda was about to launch into her lap of honour when Wideawake reared up, keeled over and died. It was one of those awful numbing moments when a tragedy is played out in front of a packed crowd.

Master Question

Master Question had the autumn season off to recover from his Badminton mishap. He was never the soundest horse, so we had to be extra cautious. I kept my hand in by taking my fiery chestnut, Copper John, to Burghley, where he gave me a blistering cross country round after a predictably rubbish dressage. I had always been slightly irked that while I was convinced he was qualified for Badminton under British Horse Society rules in 1976, Colonel Weldon begged to differ. Golden rule: you never argued with the Colonel. One year there was a German amateur (they do exist) at Celia's yard who was qualified, but whom the Colonel deemed not up to scratch for his Horse Trials. A week before the event, as a wet behind the ear, aspiring competitor, I received a call from Badminton: 'Is that young Seaman? Weldon here. You know that German fellow. Tell him he's not coming will you.'

If my junior debut coincided with my A levels, my next increasingly desperate attempt to complete Badminton came six weeks before my graduation Fashion Show at Saint Martins in 1977. It was a busy spring, honing the dressage, doing build-up competitions, printing my fabric and choosing my models and music. (The music I used was 'Purple People Eater'. I like different parts of my life to have little crossovers.)

The dressage, roads and tracks and steeplechase had miraculously gone without incident and I spent the nervous 10-minute break before the cross country sitting with other riders watching the close circuit TV and getting encouraging advice from Dick Stillwell. The talked-about fence that year was a bounce into The Lake. On the walk round many of the pundits were of the opinion the Colonel had at last lost it, and that the fence was unjumpable. There was a longer alternative over a boat house. Thank goodness for the pros. Lucinda, going first on Charles Cyzer's Killaire, bravely had a go at the bounce, not completely convinced herself that it was jumpable. Weldon one, doubters nil.

'Two minutes Mr Seaman.' A quick slug from a hunting flask and I was legged into the saddle. 'Thirty seconds.' We walked into the start box, conscious not to pick my nose in front of the TV camera. 'Three, two, one, go, good luck Mr Seaman.' 'Oh thank you,' I called back, as I heard the magic words: 'And away now Julian Seaman on Mrs Gormley's Master Question.'

For some time the tradition has been for the course to swap direction each year. In 1977 we set off right handed with a couple of welcoming obstacles before we turned left into the copse called Huntsman's Close, over a Pheasant Feeder, down a brush drop and out over a post and rails. Next was a famous old fence, The Elephant Trap, sloping poles over a yawning ditch. Once you set off on a course you get into your own little concentration bubble. The next fence, the Cirencester Rails, was a large spread. Constructed of massive timber, we nevertheless contrived to smash it to matchwood. Concentration bubble instantly popped, I hit the deck along with the horse, whose bridle had half dislodged over his ear.

I clambered back on board and trotted a few strides to check he was sound, moved back to canter and set off, somewhat shaken, to The Quarry. No damage seemed to be done and we got back into our stride. Coming soon, one after the other, were the Normandy Bank and The Lake, with its 'impossible' bounce. The Bank was all it was cracked up to be, giving me a real sense of flying as we came down from the drop.

Now I had to concentrate. For some bravado reason I had opted for the bounce route, as the fence had in fact been jumping perfectly well. There are crowds at all the fences, but The Lake is something else altogether. You ride into a gauntlet of 10,000 spectators, all secretly hoping for their money's worth.

I was suddenly aware of a bowler-hatted steward blocking my route, waving a flag, indicating me to pull up. The bubble was popped again! It transpired that the rider in front of me had broken the fence and it needed mending. Needless to say it was the boat house option which I wasn't intending to jump anyway. I then spent probably the longest 10 minutes of my life. There is a school of thought that suggests that a break like this is an advantage, as it gives the horse a breather. I would like advocates of this school to try it. As I walked in circles, trotted a bit and occasionally broke into a canter to keep Freak warmed up, several mates emerged from the crowd. Frankly I wasn't really up for light-hearted banter, but the long minutes ticked by. One mad fantasy came to mind. Eighty riders, 200,000 spectators, divide the figures and I had a fan base of 2,500!

Eventually I got the count down, the flag dropped and I rode at the bounce in cold blood. Oh how wonderful to have an honest old school master to look after you. He jumped in perfectly, splashed through The Lake, and popped neatly out over the boat. The crowd generously gave us an enormous cheer, to which I admit I rather overreacted, punching the air. I had a quick reality check as we clobbered the Whitbread Drays with all four wheels and I pulled myself together rather smartly.

There was a long gap to the next fence as the track goes over a marshy part of the park. I was over halfway round and the fates had thrown quite a lot at me already, not withstanding the three previous years of disasters. I was beginning to feel quite battle hardened. Then directly in my path to the next fence, a wall with a ditch in front, I spotted a loose dog. Competitor power took over and I shouted in no uncertain terms: 'Get that bloody dog out of the way.'

This turned out to be an ill-advised move. One dog I could have coped with, but about 30 people trying to remove said dog was a different proposition altogether. Anyway we managed to avoid all the traffic and succeeded in getting round the back loop of the course negotiating the various Vicarage Ditch fences, the Luckington Lane Crossings, the faux Grand National fences in Centre Walk and Tom Smith's Walls. Eventually there was a large brush back into the Deer Park, an enormous Log Pile and a fabulous gallop in front of Badminton House before taking a judicious pull before clearing the final fence. At last. At last. I hollered like a banshee as I rode through the finish flags.

While I was relieved and euphoric, the rest of the competition was unfolding. Lucinda's second ride was on Elaine Straker's George, on whom Elaine's son Matt had previously fallen at the last fence in 1976. Army commitments stopped him taking the ride this time and Lucinda was a somewhat reluctant pilot as George had had five falls in a row. With the confidence induced by a great round on Killaire, Lucinda gave George a superb ride, came in inside the time and went into the lead. Despite a quarter of a time fault Lucinda won her third Badminton with ease ahead of Diana Thorne and The Kingmaker, and was third with Killaire. In fourth place was Jane (Bullen) Holderness-Roddam, with her new top class ride, Warrior. My friend Alex Colquhoun had hung up his competitive boots and given the ride on his new prospect, Carawich, to Aly Pattinson. They had won Burghley in 1975, fallen at Badminton in 1976, but came an impressive fifth this year.

As a personal postscript I somehow managed to fall off in the show jumping but, despite hell and high water, I had completed my first

Badminton and had the plaque to prove it.

In the autumn of 1977, 12 of us event riders, including Richard Meade, Jane Holderness-Roddam, the then relatively unknown Ginny Holgate and show rider Georgina Simpson, (married to actor Anthony Andrews) were asked to be riders in the film *International Velvet*. The plot was a sequel to the Elizabeth Taylor 'Girl wins Grand National' film (*National Velvet*), and starred Tatum O'Neal, as an Olympic event rider, and Anthony Hopkins. In one of the real roles was 'Pup' Bullen, Jane's sister. Eventing was going to hit the big screen. In some shots Jane and her horse Warrior doubled for Tatum, which was slightly weird, as Tatum was sort of playing the role similar to Jane's real life experiences at the Mexico Olympics.

Warrior spirit

Jane Holderness-Roddam's new mount Warrior had been bought for her, by American owner Suzy Howard, from the first ever Badminton winner, John Shedden. As well as their fourth place in 1977 they had also won Burghley in 1976. Badminton was gradually becoming ever more international and Jane was one of a field of 42 from eight countries, with 32 from home, two from Ireland: John Watson and Cambridge Blue, and Helen Cantillon with Wing Forward. Two from Switzerland: Tomi Gretner with Camus Park and Joseph Burger on Clonrochen; Christian Rigal for France (Vandale B); Janusz Bobik from Poland with Tiroma; Yogi Breisner, who would become British team trainer, for Sweden with Ultimus; Valerie Wafford from the USA with Touch and Go; and for Italy, Anna Cassagrande with Daleye.

The senior guard of the British contingent included Lucinda with Village Gossip, Richard Meade with Bleak Hills, Princess Anne on

Goodwill and Mary Gordon-Watson riding Speculator. Of the young pretenders there was Tiny Clapham with her former Pony Club mount Martha, former junior Chris Bealby, Adrian Ffooks and myself on the now 14-year-old Master Question.

The weather was most odd. It had been sunny when I set off in the wagon on the Tuesday, and Andrew, my rather upmarket 'groom', who followed in his BMW had the roof down. He waved grandly as he passed us on the M4. I chuckled when the heavens opened five minutes later. More oddly though, as I was having my pipe opening gallop up Worcester Avenue, wearing my Ray-Ban shades, there was suddenly a massive snow storm!

The dressage phase was led by Warwickshire hunting girl, Jane Starkey on her 21st birthday present horse Topper Two. The cross country course was quite big and technical. As ever Frank Weldon outlined the psychology behind his course in the programme notes. He wrote: 'Badminton traditionally demands more skilful riding than anywhere else in the world.' He noted that: 'It is never good enough just to get over all the obstacles safely; to succeed at any Three Day Event, you also have to go fast.' Still keeping the faith that Badminton was a springboard to the Autumn Championships, be they Olympic, World or European, he remarked that recently, 'some of our riders had given the impression that they could have been more adventurous.'

The first couple of fences on the left-handed course as ever were designed to get competitors going. The fallen tree was followed by the log pile then a right turn to the Pardubice Taxis modelled on the Czechoslovakian Grand National's feature fence.

At the front it looked just like a simple steeplechase fence but behind it was a gaping ditch. In fact this was one for the photographers, because both horse and rider would clear the chasm without realising it was there. Next was a new version of the Cat's Cradle, with a choice of three fences in a row or two corners. Frank's advice on how to tackle the corners went thus: 'The safest way of tackling a corner is to bisect the angle, then ride on a line at right angles to the imaginary bisection and it is perhaps not so easy as it looks to hit off both correctly.'

The next was the Vicar's Choice, an almost maximum proportion open ditch in front of rails and on to the offset hedges over the Luckington Lane. Now a left turn and over a Bullfinch, a brush fence, stiff at the base, but stuffed with thin birch 10ft (3m) high designed to test the faith of horse in rider, followed by a pretend Becher's Brook. Back over the Luckington Lane, with a stone wall, a bank and a drop. The Colonel explains: 'A feature of this part of the Beaufort hunting country is the often rapid transformation from hedgerows to stone walls.' This was the idea behind this sequence of fences.

Next up was a massive parallel at the first crossing of the Vicarage Ditch. Doubling back over it, the brave route was to bisect the right angle of the ditch in front and the rail behind, and take elements A and B in one leap. The Stockholm Fence was similar to the one that Gurgle the Greek went under, but now built in such a way as to make this impossible. This was at the far end of the course almost in Wiltshire. Now it was left and over the very same Irish Bank that Golden Willow and John Shedden had taken in one in 1950. Riders jumped back into the Deer Park over a wall. Weldon said he had grouped these last three fences together on purpose for the benefit of the spectators, particularly in the Invalid Car Park.

There was a long stretch to the Whitbread Drays then The Lake. The 'in' was an upturned punt and out over a bank and rail, on the site where the 'impossible' bounce had been the year before. The Normandy Bank in this direction had a bigger drop, so the flying sensation was accentuated. At the bottom of The Ski Jump was an upright post and rail. 'Here the rider does need to exercise control and descend the bank with the horse's hocks underneath him so as to be able to loose off at the critical moment at the fence at the bottom.' It was then up a steep bank to the Faggott Pile.

There was then an opportunity to make up a bit of time before taking a pull for The Sunken Road, a rail in, drop into road, step up and rail out. At The Keeper's Rails the only thing to do was to shut your eyes and kick. There were three drop options into The Quarry followed by a very steep bank with a stone wall at the top. This was another fence that looked impossible to the layman, but horses jump surprisingly well going uphill, with their power pack behind them.

Another longish galloping stretch approached a fairly simple corner jump and then Huntsman's Grave, an 11ft 4in (3.5m) wide hole in the ground. There was a double of rails into Huntsman's Close and the Arrowhead, an angled rail over a ditch. As the course designer finally wrote: 'By now the rider's troubles are almost over for the thatched roof of The Lamb Creep and The Whitbread Bar are designed more for their visual impact but he cannot afford to relax until the last fence is jumped.'

I had come to the event really thinking that I might go quite well, despite the marathon effort of getting round in the first place. The horse deserved it, so I gave it my best shot. We were drawn 12th to go and though we had a minor misdemeanour at the fourth, we steamed round and had the rest of the day to watch how the others fared. Well into the afternoon I was somewhat astonished to hear over the loudspeakers that I was lying in third place. There were still lots of good people to go, but some of them were to rack up faults and I found myself in ninth place overnight.

In the early evening we had a few relaxing drinks in the caravan, but were surprised when Pamela Gormley, my owner, retired early to make herself a stiff black coffee. She apologised for feeling 'very funny peculiar.' We had only had a couple of drinks! It transpired later that one of the lenses of her glasses had fallen out and her world view had in consequence become somewhat impaired.

If during the night before the cross country the fences keep going through your head in a nervous progression, the night after a good round, the memory goes in a glorious mental loop till the zeds kick in.

The third day trot up is always very nerve-wracking, more so this time because Freak had nicked his foot. By this stage Andrew Day had taken responsibility for looking after my horses at big events, rightly making sure I kept out of the way. Andrew had administered to the cut, and since he was the expert, I asked him to trot the horse up instead of me. They passed the horse inspection.

After lunch there is a parade of all the horses still in the competition. As we came out of the arena Andrew noticed blood on the leg bandage. The nick had opened up again but thank goodness the horse was sound as a bell. I would be 12th to go, so there was just time to sort the nick, buy some black bandages, have some practice jumps and canter up to the Royal box to salute the Queen. As I came into the arena I was singing to myself Paul McCartney's 'With a little luck'. Show jumping was easily my worst phase, but for once it all went to plan and we jumped clear to keep our ninth place and win a replica silver horse.

Jane Holderness-Roddam won with Warrior, Lucinda was second with Village Gossip, Jane Starkey third with Topper Two. Richard Meade was sixth followed by us younger ones, Chris Bealby, Tiny Clapham and yours truly. Adrian came 15th on High Knowes.

Record champion

Another documentary crew descended on Badminton in 1979 to capture the magic of the great event. Unlike the Whitbread team in the 1960s, who had put all their eggs in Anneli Drummond-Hay's basket, with Merely a Monarch, and had pulled it off, this lot took the precaution of having two top riders to follow, each of whom had two rides. Jane Holderness-Roddam had won it the year before with Warrior and was also riding Just So and they also chose Chris Collins, the great Corinthian, who in his time had come third in the Grand National and won the Pardubice. He was entered on Gamble and Radway.

In the event Jane retired Just So on the cross country and didn't trot up Warrior on the Sunday. Chris retired Gamble after the dressage and true to form for an experienced jump jockey, fell on the steeplechase with Radway and was carted off in the ambulance. Not one of the four horses completed.

That year the competition centred round the rivalry between Lucinda and Sue Hatherly. Sue had come 11th the year before on Monacle II, a horse owned by a syndicate organised by dentist Neil Lawson-Baker. Monacle was very strong, but Sue had learned not to fight him and actually rode with a very mild rubber snaffle bit.

Round one went to Lucinda, who did the best dressage test on Killaire. Though third in 1978 the horse wasn't really built for speed, whereas Monacle, 10 points adrift in the first phase, was capable of going inside the time. Clear rounds were few and far between, but Sue set off with great confidence, had a fabulous round and duly went into the lead. Sadly for Sue this euphoria only lasted 12 minutes, because Lucinda cut every corner with Killaire and though she got 6.8 time faults, she finished 3.2 ahead of Sue. By now the show jumping penalties had been reduced from the draconian ten to five per knock-down, but Lucinda still didn't have a fence in hand. On the Sunday Sue jumped a perfect clear and rather sportingly admits to being unsporting, by wishing a hex on Lucinda. She couldn't watch, but knew it was all over when she heard the cheers congratulating the now record holding champion's fourth Badminton win.

I had thought of bringing Master Question for one last go, as he had been placed at Burghley in the autumn, but he was feeling his age a bit at home, so we redirected him to the easier Windsor Three Day Event in May, for his swansong. We just popped round for fun with no pressure, but he was still placed, and did his final show jumping round in front of the Queen again.

I had a new horse, the Reverend, who had retired from eventing until we bought him, and had become an advanced dressage horse. He was, however, qualified for Badminton. Following the usual offbeat

Seaman approach, I took him to Liphook, fell off, completed, and signed off preparation as satisfactory.

Without trying we were ninth after the dressage because of the horse, and my brush-up lessons with David Hunt, but Badminton was only my second event with him, and his second for some years. I just wanted to complete, to prove to myself I wasn't just a one horse wonder. I parted company with him twice on the way round but did complete the course. In those days Hugh Thomas had become the BBC man at the finish, and he still recalls the interview with bemusement of a bygone attitude:

'Well Julian, how was your ride?'

'Had a couple of falls and a few stops, but had great fun, super time.' Unfortunately the Rev had struck into himself and despite Andrew's best efforts it was a lost cause and we didn't trot him up the next day.

1980 saw another big entry of 68 competitors from nine countries, the most international to date, including riders from Australia, Belgium, Canada, Belgium, Spain, Ireland, USA and one unknown from New Zealand, Mark Todd and Southern Comfort. The favourites were the usual suspects of Phillips, this time with Lincoln, Lucinda on Killaire and Richard Meade on George Wimpey Ltd's Kilcashel.

The talking fence on the course was an angled foot bridge over a ditch before the Irish Bank. It required pinpoint accuracy, but the course on the whole seemed on the generous side. How wrong we were. The previous lowest percentage of riders to complete had been in the disastrous year of 1973 when only 43.48 made it round. I have to say it surprised me to find in my research that 1980 was even worse, when only 42.65 made it home.

Three weeks before the event I had been knocked unconscious and swallowed my tongue when a novice horse I was riding at a One Day Event fell on top of me after a fall at a drop fence, but little would stop me going to Badminton again. The Reverend wasn't the bravest cross country performer, but he had been placed at Burghley in the autumn, having led the dressage phase there. I had taken some long routes, which led inevitably to some people suggesting that I had become a Dressage Queen and had lost my nerve. It was only my fourth event on him and our first clear round. Could I care?!

There was a buzz among us riders out on the early phases that something was afoot. When I arrived at the steeplechase there was a log jam of about a dozen of us. An earlier competitor had broken one of the chase fences and it was taking time to fix. Lorna (Sutherland) Clarke and I had at least three ciggies while waiting our call to set off round the new figure-of-eight track.

Arriving back at the 10-minute box it was obvious there was carnage out there. Poor Lorna fell at the Footbridge and broke her leg. Former jockey Ernie Fenwick parted company from Knight Valliant five times and was hauled in front of the stewards. With his acute stutter he said: 'I'll pppplead cccconcussion'. He got a a yellow card nonetheless. Other high profile casualties included Richard Meade with Speculator, Hugh Thomas on both his rides Quality Scope and Mythic Light, Mark Phillips and Columbus, Rachel Bayliss with Gurgle the Greek, Chris Collins and Gamble and Sue Benson with Monacle. Mark Todd and Southern Comfort very nearly came to grief at the Footbridge when the horse buckled and skidded on landing, but somehow stood up unpenalised.

When I set off on the Reverend I was pleasantly surprised that he was taking a strong hold. He was feeling a better horse than ever before. I was even confident enough to take the brave route over the Footbridge, despite what it had done to more experienced combinations. He jumped it really well. After going over the Whitbread Drays, the crowd at The Lake pepped him up and he fairly tanked into it.

I'd had a longstanding superstitious tradition, instigated some years back by Adrian. We reckoned that if we went for an early morning swim in The Lake, we would not get a ducking in the afternoon. It always worked. In 1980 after our dip, an athletic Adrian loped up to the spectator fence and cleared it in one bound. I followed, only to get my toe caught in the top and come crashing down. The Reverend flew through the water only to catch his front legs coming out of the Sunken Road. I came crashing down. Spooky!

My recent concussion from three weeks ago returned and I felt quite gaga. I also noticed that the rider in front of me had crashed at the next fence and there was a hold up there. Time to stop I thought. I saw a steward approaching and, as I now know, rather flamboyantly crossed my hands and lowered my head to signal retirement. The TV announced: 'There's Julian Seaman bowing out of Badminton.' My fall and subsequent gesture was deemed suitably dramatic to feature as one of the opening clips of BBC *Grandstand* for six months. I was very flattered to discover that the same clip was part of the compilation for the last ever *Grandstand*. I am reliably informed that whatever established star might have been on the course at the same time as I was out, they always kept a camera on me, as I was likely to provide some aerobatic entertainment. One doesn't like to disappoint.

Thirty went forward to the show jumping. Poor Michael Moffett was eliminated when Red Fred dug his heels in, and all after getting round the now notorious cross country. At the top end of the survivors, Charlie Micklem made the best of his ride on Village Gossip; Richard Meade, still a force to be reckoned with, was eighth with Kilcashel; Mark was sixth on Lincoln; Sweden's Yogi Breisner was third with Ultimus; good old Killaire was second, having had one show jump down. So at his first attempt Mark Todd started a Kiwi ascendancy on Southern Comfort, whose groom was, incidentally, Andrew Nicholson, who was soon to put his stamp on the event.

Royal connection

Mark Phillips was still married to Princess Anne, when he won a sponsorship deal with the then British Leyland-owned Range Rover. This led to waggish comments about one state industry sponsoring another. His placing the previous year on the company's Lincoln was largely because of the mayhem on the course. Mark found the horse quite a difficult ride but it was with this sort of challenge that he excelled as a rider. His dual winner Great Ovation was not the most genuine horse, and Columbus had proved too strong for the Princess to hold. Though they stood about a quarter the way down the record entry of 80 competitors from 10 countries they set off boldly round the course, where the going was getting quite sticky after some rain. Posting the fastest time of the day they moved up from 19th to take the overnight lead.

My former Pony Club team friend Tiny Clapham was now riding a horse with serious international potential, an impressive grey called Windjammer. She also had a pet horse at home, called Bowbrook, which she was going to point to point for fun. Her trainer was Dick Stillwell, who also used to run an annual show jumping course, pre-Badminton at the Russells' place at Wylye. Wylye, in those days was used as the training launch pad for each year's championship team. It was, in its heyday, a Mecca of equestrian training under the watchful eye of the formidable, wheelchair bound, Lady Hugh Russell.

Dick's course was always fun, and I needed any help in that phase that I could get. I had known Dick for years, so signed up. The Russells' always had superb cooks and it was all very civilised. On the application form there was a box to tick if we wanted a groom for the duration. Naturally I did. However when I arrived, Lady Hugh informed me that I could jolly well 'do' my own horse, and then announced to us all that dinner would be at eight sharp. I made an embarrassing show of being a useless boy, and turned up to dinner late, covered in straw and feigning distress. I got my groom the next morning.

Dick was nervous about his protégé, Tiny, risking herself race riding. I was going to Badminton as an also-ran for my last attempt to complete on a second horse, so Dick suggested she put me up, as 'a man of lesser consequence.' I had one ride round Tweseldown that year, which kicked off an eight-year race riding jaunt.

Tiny duly came sixth at Badminton and went on to take eighth place as an individual at the European Championships at Horsens in Denmark. Of the other placings Ginny Holgate, a former Junior European Champion, was back in the big time, having nearly lost an arm through an appalling break some years back. She was eighth with Priceless. In fifth was the now successful Irish racehorse trainer Jessie Harrinton and Amoy. Yogi Breisner was fourth and Richard Meade third. Lying in second going into the show jumping was Hawaiian American Sandy Pfleuger, whose cottage in Chobham I occasionally stayed at while riding my horse from Gracious Pond Stables, Mincing Lane (really!). Sandy had two down with Free Scott, easing the pressure on Mark with Lincoln. He now had a bit of leeway but rolled one too. Phillips took the trophy though to become only the second person after Lucinda to do so four times. He later married Sandy.

In the old days we assumed qualifications for horse and rider were for life. This was not to be. 1981 was going to be my last serious event. I had no new event horses in the pipeline, and had decided that the Foxhunters at Aintree was to be my next goal. I was all organised for Badminton, so was rather taken aback when I got a call from the director of Horse Trials, Colonel Peter Hodgson: 'Julian old boy, I don't think you are qualified.'

The Reverend had been a bit lacklustre in the spring and Andrew nearly persuaded me to give it a miss. Somewhat to my surprise though, the horse gave me a great feel schooling at Tweseldown, so I was up for it. Peter's call was a bit of a shock. Right up to the Monday of the event I had no idea whether I was going or not. By this stage I was old and bold enough to phone Frank Weldon and ask him what the form was. 'Oh alright, come along then,' he replied. That rather neatly squared the circle. He hadn't let me run five years previously with Copper John, who probably was qualified, but would let me bring the Rev, who probably wasn't. As ever, what Weldon said, went.

It was strange going round the roads and tracks knowing that it would certainly be the last time. To be honest it was a bit of a relief. We didn't exactly cover ourselves in glory, but had the satisfaction of mission accomplished, by completing the event and earning my third plaque.

PART 4

A CHANGE OF DIRECTION (1982–2001)

There for the beer

For eight years running every spring had been geared to a competitive build up to Badminton. It was very strange to be a retired event rider at 26, with some considerable mileage on the clock, but I was going to go and have fun as a spectator. Any regrets were dispelled on the Monday before the event, as I had somehow managed to win a point to point on Tiny's Bowbrook.

I had also been allowed to park my caravan in the competitors' park, so I was with all my friends and 'there for the beer'. For some years now I had been a public address commentator at One Day Events and had always fancied my chances of doing some TV work. The BBC had been well staffed with legends such as Dorian Williams and Raymond Brooks-Ward. The new boys were Hugh Thomas and Mike Tucker, who was still riding at this level. The producer in those days was Fred Viner, who very kindly let me have a go while they were off air. The technique for TV is very different to PA commentary, for the rather obvious reason that your audience can see what is going on. What is required is 'colour' and opinion, rather than factual information. This wasn't an audition, but great fun, and stood me in good stead some years later.

Tracy, my girlfriend at the time, who I had met when she was grooming in Chobham, was by now working as a nanny for a rather grand banking family, who had a company house in Chelsea Square. Coincidently they had hired a weekend cottage in Wiltshire the same weekend as the event.

I had kept in touch with Georgina Andrews (Simpson) since *International Velvet* days, designing some head scarves for the Piccadilly store. She and Anthony Andrews, who was the national heartthrob at the time with *Brideshead Revisited* in full flow, were staying in Bath for the Trials. They asked Tracy and me out for the evening. I don't think the Chelsea gang quite got over the fact that their nanny was being whisked off to have dinner with Sebastian Flyte.

The competition that was distracting my social life was unfolding. Rachel Bayliss, as expected, led the dressage with Mystic Minstrel, but Richard Meade was only four points adrift on Speculator III, a ride he had taken over from Mary Gordon-Watson the previous year, coming a modest 32nd. Less than two points behind Meade was Bruce Davidson with JJ Babu. Rachel picked up some time faults and had one down in the jumping. The final result was a second win for Richard. Meanwhile Bruce had improved on his previous best to take second slot, and Rachel finished a very happy third, admitting that the Badminton atmosphere always got to her and affected her performance.

Ginny Holgate was making her mark with fourth on Priceless and Sue Benson was next with the mare Gemma Jay. Since the last Badminton Lucinda had become Mrs David Green, but David would not be overshadowed. He came sixth with Mairangi Bay, while Lucinda came seventh and eighth with Regal Realm and Beagle Bay.

For many years Badminton has made charitable donations, but in 1983 as well as supporting The British International Equestrian Fund – the body set up to cover the expense of sending all three equestrian teams, dressage, show jumping and eventing, to the Los Angeles Olympics 18 months hence – the Horse Trials also supported the British Fields Sports Society, which, before the Countryside Alliance, was at the forefront of the fight to combat the threat to hunting. Two fences, the Aintree tribute ones in Centre Walk, were dedicated to the Grand National Appeal. Twenty-six years down the line British Teams were being funded largely through Sports Grants, the hunting act had been passed, though there was still lobbying for a repeal, but the Grand National had unequivocally been saved.

The course in 1983 probably had more alternative fences to enable the lesser lights to make the trip, but those wanting to make an impression on the selectors, not just for the up and coming European Championships at Frauenfeld in Switzerland but also the following Olympic Games, had some formidable direct routes to take on.

Trouble was quite evenly spread around the course and as ever some of the more experienced riders came to grief, sometimes at seemingly innocuous or familiar obstacles.

Denmark's Nils Haagensen, who had won the alternative Equestrian Games at Fontainebleau in 1980, had a stop at the third in Huntsman's Close and jumped so big into The Quarry that Nils was dislodged from the saddle. (Fontainebleau was set up because there had been a partial boycott of the Moscow Olympics because of the Soviet invasion of Afghanistan, which seems worth a thought years down the line.) Rachel Bayliss had led the dressage again with Mystic Minstrel, but fell on the Saturday at the Park Wall, which had never knowingly caused any trouble before.

Mark Phillips paid the penalty when Classic Lines didn't produce the asked for bounce at The Pig Sties and put his rider on the floor.

At the Bull Pens David Green went airborne when Mairangi Bay clobbered one element, landed like a circus act across the saddle, jumped the next element like a trick rider and bit the dust. Tom Smith's Walls, an old feature fence on the far side of the Luckington Lane, on the way home tripped up both Marje Comerford and Cheale Harvester and Charlotte Steel with The Bailiff.

Tiny Clapham had an annoying 20 penalties when a trip coming out of The Lake made the next jump impossible, and overboldness caused Ginny Holgate and Night Cap II to fault coming up and out over The Quarry.

Laura Tierney, whose mother had trained me with my novice horses, had the unbelievable frustration of having a great round on Kingsbridge Kip spoiled by a stop at the roofed final fence for the second year running.

The fence to give riders night-before collywobbles was The New Moon, a massive timber upright at the foot of a slope. In fact if the horses took off where they were meant to, it wasn't that big. Yet another Weldon optical illusion to impress the crowd, terrify the riders and give the horses a nice jump.

Only two riders got inside the time, Jessie Harrington with Amoy who finished third, and the winner for the fifth time, Lucinda Green on Regal Realm. Mike Tucker had his moment in the sun with General Bugle coming second, Lorna Clarke was fourth with Danville, achieving the sole clear round in the show jumping. Lucinda had another one up her sleeve, however, coming fifth with Beagle Bay.

For the first time I could remember, I hardly spent any time at the event. I went down to walk the course on the Friday but that was it. A close family friend had a wedding on the Saturday, and on the Sunday I flew to Hamburg to set up a stand for my father's company at an industrial trade fair. It was quite cathartic.

A new era

Orwell's year was another wilderness one for me. The point to pointing had been coming along, but I had broken my collarbone quite badly in the February. Tiny, who had also injured herself, and I were asked by Martin Whiteley (the former owner of The Poacher), now a House Master at Eton, to come and have dinner and give a talk to the Eton Equestrian Association on 1 March. I don't suppose we were much of an advertisement for equestrian sports, all bandaged up and hobbling!

In the history of Badminton there is a noticeable pattern of eras moving on. Weldon ceded to Willcox, she to Meade, Meade to Phillips, Phillips to Prior-Palmer. Lucinda was to have one more shout, but a new group of pretenders was forming.

Another era had also ended. The 10th Duke of Beaufort, referred to as 'Master', had died in February of the year, and Mr David Somerset had succeeded as the 11th Duke.

In 1984 Lucinda led from the front, doing the best dressage with Beagle Bay and not accumulating another fault all weekend. She had achieved the incredible feat of winning the world's most famous event six times on six different horses. Beagle Bay had looked a contender coming fifth the previous year, though he had been difficult to keep sound, despite winning at Burghley in 1981. Lucinda had also taken the ride back on Village Gossip and ended up fifth on him. Lorna Clarke was still racking up placings, coming fourth on Danville and at this stage the rider who had completed Badminton most times. Lorna had a unique style of riding cross country, seemingly doing the whole trip with a completely loose rein, achieving a remarkable lack of interference with her horses.

Though arguably outshone by Lucinda's sixth win, a new sensation had arrived in the shape of Scotsman Ian Stark. On his debut he came third on Oxford Blue and sixth with Sir Wattie. Mark Todd was back, proving that his 1980 win on Southern Comfort wasn't a fluke. This time the 6ft 3in (1.90m) rider arrived with the unlikely conveyance of the 15.3hh Charisma. They had been unbeaten in New Zealand, and Mark was still determined to realise his dreams of riding at the Olympics. They achieved the second best dressage test and added nothing to it. Of course their prayers were answered in Los Angeles when they took individual gold. In LA the USA took team gold but the British team of Ginny with Priceless, Lucinda with Regal Realm, Ian on Oxford Blue and Tiny with Windjammer took the silver.

Since the publication of *Horse Laughs* in 1983 I had taken to doing quite a bit more writing. The original idea for the book had come from Adrian's mother, who had suggested that between us we had experiences, contacts and a healthy sense of the ridiculous about our sport. Adrian had hung up his boots, but I was still riding when we started doing our research. We arranged meetings with the great and the good and found ourselves having some very jolly lunches. But how would we regiment all the anecdotes? Actually we found out quite quickly that for many of the yarns to have any resonance you probably needed to have been there. We still carried on, and cobbled together a manuscript of sorts but it sat around at agents for weeks on end.

Adrian decided to drop out of things and went to India for a year and gave me his blessing to go it alone with a revamp. *Horse Laughs* was a pick and mix of facts, cartoons, weird photos, gossip and spoofs in the style of *Private Eye* magazine. My editor correctly described it as a 'bed and bogside' book, a technical publishing term I gather. Though it was a bit niche and became a bit dated, it went quite well and encouraged me to give the same treatment to show jumping and horse racing in *Showing Off* and *Turfed Out*.

1969 runner-up Angela Martin-Bird's brother Alastair had set up a video company in the early 1980s and had secured the rights to make programmes for sale of Badminton and Burghley. He could use BBC footage but film his own links. He asked me to write, direct and voice his first attempt at Burghley 1984, which was a steep learning curve to say the least. Badminton 1985 was my second attempt.

I got down to Badminton early on the Monday morning, the earliest day I had ever turned up there, not least because I had to dump the caravan and get into Bristol for 11am, for an interview with BBC radio to plug the paperback version of my first book. I had also just been signed up as a columnist on a new magazine *Horse Weekly*.

As what was to be a one-off approach, I thought I would edit the cross country as if the viewer was a spectator, standing at each fence in order, and seeing several go over it, showing different ways of tackling the obstacle. A bit too clever perhaps? Anyway it was great because I was back at Badminton and actually doing something.

I needed a bit of a boost because my debut attempt at the Aintree Foxhunters in April had ended with a fall at the first fence.

Torrance Watkins Fleischmann and Finvarra did the best test for the USA in 1985 but Mark Todd and Charisma were only a quarter of a point behind. Ginny was next with Night Cap followed by Richard Walker with Accumulator, who subsequently retired on the cross country. Ginny's assault was two pronged, as hot on the heels of those four was her other ride, Priceless. All the top combinations, bar Walker, went well cross country, though of that group only Priceless and

Charisma came inside the time. The only other rider to do the same was Mary Thomson on Divers Rock.

Toddy, runner up the previous year, with an impeccable show jumping round, was overnight leader. Ginny and Priceless were clear. When the traditional groan from the crowd went up, the Holgate era had begun.

Ginny was also third with Night Cap. Mary Thomson, a former pupil of Sheila Willcox was seventh, Lorna Clarke was still totting up completions with both Myross ninth and Glentrool 13th, and in 15th place was Madeleine Gurdon, who would become Lady Lloyd-Webber.

Boggy Badminton

The heavens opened again in 1986, and when the course is wet, predictions about who will do well often go by the board. This of course is one of the most difficult tasks facing a course designer. In perfect conditions they don't want half the field to go round clear inside the time, but if conditions are tough they want to avoid disaster. Certainly in wet years the official relativity of the three phases gets skewed and the cross country, rightly the most influential, takes on even greater significance.

Even so, to be involved in the final shake up, a decent dressage gets you off in the right spirit. Bruce Davidson and JJ Babu led this phase from Ginny and Night Cap and Ian Stark with Sir Wattie. The going was so sticky however, that not a single combination got round without time penalties. If ever there was a year to pull up from an indifferent dressage with as fast a cross country as possible, this was it.

Drawn in 18th place in the starting order was Rachel Hunt at her second Badminton with Piglet II. They had been no better than 26th

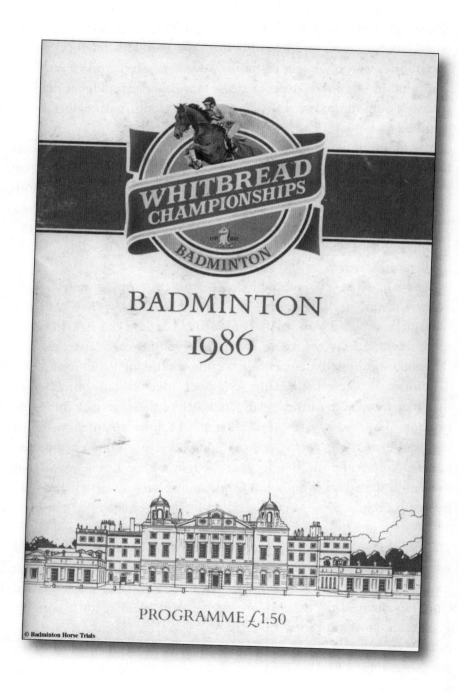

the year before. They were 46th of 60 before the endurance phase, where some riders were even getting time penalties on the steeplechase. She probably had a couple of advantages going quite early on. The ground was less cut up, and the scale of the problems that the course would cause wouldn't have yet let gloom permeate the 10-minute box.

She set off in determined mode and went clear in the fastest time of the day to rise in spectacular fashion to second place. There were few jumping clears on the cross country, unsurprisingly including those who filled the top three slots. Ian Stark emerged triumphant with Sir Wattie with easily enough in hand to accommodate one down in the jumping. Rachel held on to her second spot and Rodney Powell took third with Pomeroy.

There had been a potential disaster on the cross country. Polly Schwerdt and her diminutive Dylan had been favourites with the equestrian press. Dylan was setting off to become the first horse to complete the event five times on the trot, so to speak. After jumping the first they clipped the back of a rogue car crossing the course. Polly dismounted to assess the damage and decided to carry on, though they had a stop at the subsequent fence before they got back into their rhythm. The drama was one of those bubble-bursting moments which are so hard to refocus from. Also because it had happened between fences, no jump judge had thought to time her delay, so that she could have had time penalties deducted on appeal. Fortunately no lasting damage had been done and they jumped clear the next day, finishing 14th.

I was there from the Wednesday with Alastair's crew and as ever stayed in the caravan, which at boggy Badmintons is somewhat primitive. My father, however, still had a room at the Petty France Hotel, so a bath and a decent dinner were available. For some reason I still got an invitation to the cocktail party on the Thursday. It is an institution in itself. The Duke and Duchess, both the previous one and the current 11th Duke, greet every one of what must be 500 guests.

In the early days the dressage arena was in front of the house and one of the public car parks was between the house and The Lake.

Hailing a cab in flying form, Lt. Col. J.D. Crawford and Steadfast III in 1951.

The military origins of the sport were still very much in evidence in Badminton's early years. Switzerland's Otto Schwarz came eighth in 1951 with Euphrona.

Badminton's first winner, John Shedden and Golden Willow flies a fence in hunting style.

Sheila Willcox won the event three times in a row from 1957 to 1959. She was also an early mentor to future winner Mary King.

David Somerset, the 11th Duke of Beaufort, came second at Badminton in 1959, riding Countryman III.

Former Grand National jockey, chairman of junior selectors and early Assistant Director of Badminton, the splendid Col. 'Babe' Moseley.

Director Hugh Thomas at The Lake celebrating the event's 50th anniversary with a copy of the poster for the first running in 1949.

The legendary Col. Frank Weldon, former winner, but best known for his designing genius. He built courses 'To frighten the life out of the riders, but be fair to the horses.'

In 1953 a European Championships was held at Badminton. Here, Sweden's John Asker and Iller jump back into the deer park over a wall, which was part of the course until 1977.

Bowler hatted Mrs J. Engleman on Fanfayre.

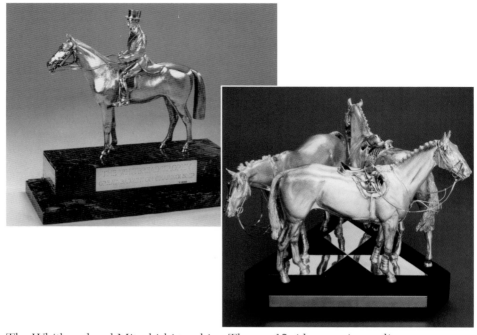

The Whitbread and Mitsubishi trophies. The top 12 riders receive replicas.

Lucinda Green, who won on six different horses, displays her characteristic lower leg position on Beagle Bay.

Ginny Elliot and Mary King continued to prove that women and men competed on equal terms by winning the world's greatest event.

The Royal Family has always had close links to Badminton. Queen Mary stayed there during WW II and the Queen was also a regular visitor to the event. She is pictured here with the 10th Duke of Beaufort and the Duke of Edinburgh.

Princess Anne was encouraged by Sir John Miller to take up eventing and became European Champion. She was also a silver medallist on Goodwill, here jumping at Badminton over the Ski Jump.

When the Queen's horse Columbus proved too strong a ride for Princess Anne, Mark Phillips took over the ride to win in 1974.

Zara Phillips emulated her mother by becoming European Champion and also became World Champion before completing Badminton in 2008.

Narrow, aiming fences like this one out of The Lake test the skill of today's riders, like Caroline Powell with Leanamore.

The long trench, known as the Vicarage Ditch, has provided many complex designs to snake over and test accuracy and nerve. Here, clearing it well are Jane Swallow and Bellyquinn.

The Normandy Bank was a 'wow factor' jump. Spectacular to ride and great for spectators and photographers, it was not that difficult an obstacle. Future TV commentator Mike Tucker is shown here with General Bugle.

The thrill of eventing does entail risk. Neither horses nor riders were hurt in these spectacular spills, but the pictures demonstrate that a ride round Badminton is not just a walk in the park. Top, Gillian Maybury and Rum Tum Tugger. Bottom, Pascal Leroy and Glenburny du Leu.

The author on Master Question in 1978 at the Stockholm Fence. They finished ninth.

The author about to take an early shower. This was the prang that featured in the BBC *Grandstand* intro clips for six months.

A glimpse of the media centre at press conference time.

Competitors briefing in Badminton Village Hall.

The fabulous old stables where the equine contestants are housed.

Former champion Pippa Funnell lets her dogs examine the alternative route at The Lake.

New Zealander Andrew Nicholson has completed Badminton a record 26 times.

New Zealand's Mark Todd, arguably the best event rider ever, is pictured winning from the front on his chance ride, the Bevan's Horton Point.

These comprise the army of volunteers, like jump judges, riders and their other halves, owners and the great and good of Beaufortshire, the term given to hunt-following locals.

Over the years I have worked out the ideal way to position myself at this excellent party. I briefly outlined the method some years ago in my book *Sixteen Hands Between Your Legs*, but it bears repeating in case you find yourself there one day. The whole of the ground floor is in use, with marquees erected for the overspill. In clement years we also go out on to the back lawn. First tip is to introduce yourself to the waitress who gives you your first glass of champagne. Then select a doorway to loiter near. There may be dozens of your friends at the party, but you are most likely to see them by staying in one spot yourself. Also the waitress knows where you are to keep topping up your glass. Take it from a professional, the system works! One waitress turned out to be one of my Saint Martins' students.

Making the film was drenching, but, being part of the media outfit we had 'all area' vehicle passes and did shots of the usually ignored phases of roads and tracks and steeplechase. For obvious reasons only the occasional nanosecond clip appeared in the BBC broadcast coverage, but we had the luxury of making a more relaxed programme, giving the whole picture of the event as it unfolded. We used Hugh Thomas to do the links.

We also had more time to analyse the fences. Much of this filming we did on the Wednesday and Thursday, while the competitors were walking the course. Since the majority of riders were friends of mine, we often had to do several takes, as they would blow the shot by flicking a gesture or uttering an oath. On live telly you can go into McCririck mode and bluff it. For a recorded programme there is no excuse for bloopers, so we often had to 'go again'. It was good media training though, and was to be useful some years later. Being back and involved brought some strange emotions. Eventing is a very close-knit community, and though everyone is competitive, we all care for friendly rivals in what is most certainly a risk sport. Even having stopped riding, as the cross country approached I found myself getting really quite nervous for the competitors and relieved when it was all over.

It would be two years before we all returned, as the spring of 1987 was so wet that the event had to be abandoned long before anyone had thought of setting off for Gloucestershire.

Weldon bows out

After the appallingly wet Badminton of 1986 and the abandonment the following year, it was eventually decided to move the event to the first week of May. This had two obvious benefits. First, there was a half reasonable chance that the weather would be better, and second, riders would have an extra month to prepare. The April date had always been very early in a spring season which only began in mid March. Wordsworth would have been upset, however. In April Badminton House was surrounded by a fabulous sea of daffodils and Huntsman's close was carpeted with bluebells.

1988 was also Frank Weldon's last as director. He was 74 years old, and had decided to call it a day. I had been reporting on some events for *Horse & Hound* magazine and was very honoured to be asked to write the Colonel's valedictory. I reprint it in full:

FRANK WELDON is the master of knowing just what a horse can do. Julian Seaman looks back on the career of Badminton's director for 25 years, whose retirement brings the end of an era . . .

Though a Whitbread Championships at Badminton without Frank Weldon at the helm seems almost inconceivable, there was bound to come a time when he decided to stand down. Since he is in his 75th year there was obviously speculation as to who was going to succeed him. He has always made it plain that he feels no need for an understudy 'hanging around in the background' but concedes that course designers capable of filling his shoes 'don't grow on trees'.

It was only when Hugh Thomas announced his intention to leave BEP (British Equestrian Promotions), with no particular future plans, that the ideal candidate became available. Wanting Hugh to take over at a young age, Frank Weldon decided to retire in this Olympic year and hand over the reins.

Before the war his first love was racing. He was successful in hunter chases and between the flags, but suffered a major disappointment when qualification changes prevented him from achieving his ambition of riding in the Grand National. To some extent this would explain why he has little sympathy for those who keep just getting squeezed out of Badminton as the qualifications increase.

NEW FANGLED

After the war, during which he spent time in Colditz, he returned to soldiering and became CO of the King's Troop, Royal Horse Artillery.

He was introduced to the 'new fangled' sport of Three Day Eventing almost by chance. He felt that his men needed some form of equestrian competition, but racing was financially out of the question: 'They wouldn't have had the price of a 30-bob theatre ticket between them', so something else was needed.

At a dinner party his General suggested the horse trials at Badminton; a subaltern was dispatched to get a schedule and four of them entered. Weldon spent a week in Tetbury Cottage Hospital as a result!

Undaunted, he saw this new sport as ideal for his recently retired racehorse Kilbarry, with whom he proceeded to win the European Championships at Windsor in 1955 and Badminton in

1956, led a succession of triumphant teams and won a team gold medal and individual bronze at the Stockholm Olympic Games.

He also became the most widely travelled judge and technical delegate on the international eventing circuit – a position he retained until a couple of years ago, when the lure of the airport departure lounge had lost its sparkle.

After the spectacular successes of the 1950s, British eventing hit the doldrums. Public interest faded and our teams were failing. The final ignominy was at the Tokyo Games, where Great Britain, Japan and Korea were the only teams to be eliminated.

Although Badminton was instigated by the 10th Duke to prepare British teams for competition abroad, by now it was singularly failing to do this. British riders were coming across fences the like of which they have never seen before. The Duke's heir David Somerset, who had previously come second at Badminton, moved to the estate and asked Frank, with his wealth of international knowledge, to design the course in 1965. Two years later the Colonel also took on the role of director.

Almost immediately he started introducing 'foreign' jumps to the course, many of these are now feature fences: the Normandy Bank ('They all thought I'd kill the lot of them with that'), the Horsens Bridge, the Pardubice Taxis, the Stockholm Fence, the Fairbanks Bounce and the Frauenfeld Platform. He modified his borrowed ideas to the Gloucestershire countryside and also invented many ideas of his own, most notably the bounce and the annual technical puzzles by the park Ha-ha.

He has found his riding experiences essential and is a master of knowing just what a horse can do. His courses have deliberately become more technical as horsemanship has improved, but he always sticks to his Weldonism of 'frightening the life out of the riders without hurting the horses.'

As he explains, the 'legal' dimensions of the jumps have not altered since the Olympics of 1912, but clever siting and modern aides like JCB diggers can easily alter terrain. The Normandy Bank was constructed from rubble when the M4 was being built.

Frank Weldon had lived and hunted in the Beaufort country for many years and his local connections were undoubtedly a help in securing the army of helpers needed. The Whitbread Championships almost feel like the Beaufort Hunt's private competition and all the officials guard their jobs jealously.

But Badminton today is not just about riders. It is a massive public spectacle – a point which Frank always reiterates at the competitors' briefing: 'The public have paid their money; it is their day out, not yours. If it wasn't for them you wouldn't be here.'

With the annual crowd of a quarter of a million there are many other things to worry about. The traffic system is always being improved and regular spectators know to stagger their arrival and departure. The loos are a considerable expense and, as always happens with large crowds, there are bound to be trouble makers. Recently the catering companies altered the licensing times to try and minimise the problem.

ROYAL VISITS

The royal interest definitely helped to put Badminton on the map, but it now has a life of its own. Sadly in these days of security risks, the Queen's informal visits, often sitting on an overcoat by a fence, have been restricted, so she tends to come less frequently.

Because he is in charge of the ultimate event course, Frank Weldon has become to some a 'bogey man', which one suspects he rather likes. His military style enhances this image, but the glimpses of his twinkly smile reveals the humour behind some of his more chauvinistic remarks.

He usually greets overseas riders at the briefing with the words 'You foreigners at the back, do you understand what I'm saying?'

He refers to the easier options at his fences as the 'bumblepuppy routes' and has never made a secret of the fact that he doesn't approve of women in international teams. He hastens to add that he thinks they are just as brave as men and equally accomplished (in some obvious cases more so), but when things go wrong they 'shed a little tear'.

Frank also spent many years as an equestrian journalist. When, in the early days of eventing, it was mentioned to him that the sport was not getting any coverage, but show jumping was, he wrote it up himself, spending two years with the *Observer* and then about 20 with the *Sunday Telegraph*. He also wrote extensively on eventing for *Horse & Hound*.

All his experiences would make a marvellous book, but he claims he has no intention of writing one. He also has no intention of shadowing Hugh as a consultant, though he says 'the old fool will still be around if they want to ask me anything'.

1988 sees the end of an era. Frank Weldon's immense contribution, not just to Badminton but to the whole sport of Three Day Eventing, can probably never be equalled.

For the first time that year *Horse & Hound* asked me to do a form guide as the Tote had opened a book on the competition. As I wrote: 'Unlike racing, where horses and trainers seem to get publicity at the expense of jockeys, in eventing it is the riders rather than the horses who are household names and who usually play the significant role in the horses' preparation.

Badminton, however, is like the Grand National in that the very best horses will probably finish at the top, with the other prizes going to good Three Day Event horses rather than the one day specialists.'

Here is what I wrote about some of the main protagonists:

Volunteer, Tinks Pottinger: To make doubly sure of a replica Whitbread silver horse, Mrs Pottinger could go very close to winning on this experienced 11 year old. The more international riders at Badminton the better and no one would begrudge another New Zealand victory. (They finished fourth.)

Friday Fox, Rachel Hunt: Another quite old horse at 13, this skewbald mare brings back happy memories of Lorna Clarke's Popadom. If Rachel ever achieves Lorna's remarkable consistency – which she could – there will have been two coloured 'circus ponies' to create stars. This one probably won't win, and Badminton is a major step up from the previous medals and prizes from junior and Young Rider European championships and Stockholm, but they could go well. (Seventh)

Sir Wattie, Ian Stark: Ian Stark made history by being the first person to win Badminton wearing a crash helmet (head gear rules had changed the year before) and pink coat. The combination are reigning champions here and serious contenders for Seoul. Few people have won these trials on the same horse, but it could happen this time. (Winner)

Glenburnie, Ian Stark: This horse is ridden by a retired DHSS clerk in his retirement, however the rider has won a team silver medal at the Los Angeles Olympics, team gold medals at every international championship since, and Badminton to boot. Having achieved all that he rightly can't understand why he isn't a 'star' – he's far too nice! Not his top ride but could go quite well. (Second)

Murphy Himself, Ginny (Holgate) Leng: One hell of a puller but a joy to watch. Murphy won at Burghley in 1986 and was later off for a season, but if all goes well he could win. He will have the backing not only of his rider but one of the most efficient behind the scenes organisations ever seen in this sport. (Too strong, fell and retired.)

Horton Point, Ros Bevan: Previously taught by the maestro of Gleneagles (Mark Phillips), being the first Range Rover scholar at Gatcombe, Ros should have a decent ride on this horse and if she is lucky could end up in the frame. (Ninth)

Master Craftsman, Ginny Leng: The horse's name could refer to the rider. Master Craftsman, second in Stockholm last year has yet to taste the big time, but with Ginny riding has every chance of winning – if she doesn't beat herself on her other more experienced mount. (Third)

For the record my 1/2/3 predictions were: Master Craftsman; Volunteer; Sir Wattie, and the Tote odds were 8-1 Master Craftsman; 9-1 Sir Wattie; 10-1 Murphy Himself and Glenburnie, so for once the tipsters and professionals weren't far out.

Ian made history with his first and second place, and had at last become the 'star' that his performances had merited. Master Craftsman looked a class act in the making, and with good weather there weren't any great surprises. However, Ginny decided that Murphy was too much of a handful for her after her fall at The Ski Jump. She brokered a swap with Ian for his chestnut Griffin, a deal which Ginny almost immediately regretted. Despite having won Burghley, Murphy probably was too strong for her and suited Ian's swashbuckling style, but Griffin wasn't in the same league. Also making his first, and successful return to Badminton was my former Pony Club colleague Brynley Powell, who managed 19th with Spiderman III.

1988 was quite emotional for me, as in April I had eventually managed to lurch my way round the Grand National course in the Foxhunters. For the record I had wiped out at the first fence three times, on, or rather off, three different horses. With some sense of achievement, but mainly relief, I had decided to hang up my boots, something which I had ritualistically and literally done in the hall of my home in London. Since I had never professed to be a race riding jockey, my horses had probably not really achieved their full potential, so to improve their sale price we put up a top point to point man, Jonny Portman, on my second string at a meeting on Badminton Saturday. Mission accomplished. He won.

I had been a bit demob happy during the week, and as usual went out to supper each night. On the Friday I returned quite late to the stable annex of the Petty France Hotel. I pushed the short-timer light button to find the keyhole of my room. All hell then broke loose. I had somehow set off the fire alarm. I had to do much grovelling in the breakfast dining room on the Sunday morning.

It had been a good Badminton, which was even more appreciated after the event's cancellation the previous year.

Ginny's glory

Between being appointed and starting the job at Badminton, Hugh Thomas had the dry run of designing the course for the Seoul Olympics. He had started his course designing at a very young age, putting up the only Pony Club course I ever failed to complete, on his family farm at South Warnborough, Hampshire. He then went on to design the Three Day Event course on the Scott's estate at Rotherfield Park. This was used for three junior and two Young Riders European Championships.

For several years I had been doing the fence illustrations for the programmes at many events, and Rotherfield was one of them. They had also previously asked me to design a logo for the event, so I modestly used myself riding all three phases as the model. For the YR Championships in 1985 the design was cast for the medals. My irreverent friends, mocking my artistic proclivities, suggested that here was another Queen on a coin.

Since Hugh's Seoul job was by nature long distance, he commissioned me to do 'artist's impressions' of the jumps so that his technical instructions would take on a more 'real' appearance. Unfortunately a couple of times the course builders took my perspective a bit too literally and laid out the ground lines at an angle to the jumps! Hugh still recalls this with amusement.

Because of the Olympics Hugh could only really concentrate on Badminton from the autumn of 1988, but in his first year wasn't going to make too many changes. Many of the Badminton obstacles had become traditional and iconic ambitions of each generation of rider, though the Colonel used to tweak them to stop riders getting complacent. (To the best of my knowledge no rider has ever been complacent setting off round Badminton.) Hugh wasn't starting from scratch, and was able to find his feet as both director as well as designer. Badminton has been unique in combining the roles up to now.

His first course would have given him confidence, as 22 jumped round clear with only three inside the time. There were no eliminations on the course, as the mindset of riders seemed to be changing. After two stops at an obstacle, they eschewed the final attempt, and, as the old school might put it, gave up, or in modern parlance, retired. Ten took this option.

At the top end of the competition, Ian had gelled with Murphy Himself and finished fifth. He was also fourth on Glenburnie. Mark Todd had taken a last minute ride on Rodney Powell's The Irishman, as Rodney had broken a collarbone the weekend before, and cruised into third place, inside the time. Mary King felt hard done by in the dressage as one judge consistently marked her down on King Boris and she lost the Championship by less than the cost of a show jump to a final clear round by Ginny Leng and Master Craftsman.

I have been lucky enough to have been out hunting as a guest of the Beaufort once or twice. Once Cub Hunting on an ex-chaser of Viscount Petersham's called Rollercoaster, who was by then with the

Darlings at Hullavington. Another time I had been at the Beaufort Hunt Ball and due to go out the next day when I was told that my horse was lame. I was taken through to a very senior table, where I was introduced to an improbably Grande Beaufortshire Dame: 'My dear boy, I'll mount you.' Woahh there! I had a great day, not least because we spent some time in Badminton Park, jumped the hedges in Centre Walk, hunted by Huntsman's Close and cooled down in The Lake.

On another occasion my car had broken down on the way to Gloucestershire. I was able to limp it to the farmer who kept our hunters and hitched a lift the rest of the way with my sister. This left me stranded in the country on the Sunday evening. 'No problem,' said one of the Darlings' house guests, 'My helicopter is picking me up from the Badminton air strip tomorrow. Would you like a lift?' Bless the car for packing up! The last time I went out was in 1989, when for a short time I was hunting correspondent for *Country Life*. I stayed the night before with huntsman Ian Farquhar, which proved dangerous as it was his birthday, but I had the fun of riding a couple of hunt horses.

That year also saw a new venture in the equestrian lecture circuit. Photographer Kit Houghton decided that instead of the usual cold indoor riding school venues, he would use his vast library of slides to put on a theatre tour with Badminton Champion Ginny Leng. I was commissioned to write the script and organise the music and sound effects. We went on the road, and because of our star, received considerable acclaim.

Behind the mike

Some years back I had done a little bit of TV voiceover for a pony series on the now defunct TV AM. The competition consisted of a mix between a Gymkhana and a horse trial, with 'apple bobbing', cross

country and also some dressage with music. This was held at an establishment called Wellington Riding, where for many years I had done PA
commentary at their events. I was also asked to judge the musical
dressage with the 1970s pop star Alvin Stardust. The winner of this
made-for-TV nonsense was a nine-year-old called Lucy Wiegersma.

Having made and voiced several Badminton and Burghley videos, I
was more than pleased to get a call on the Tuesday of Badminton 1990
from Sky/Eurosport asking me to be one of their live commentators for
the weekend. Realistically I was unlikely to get a chance with the
established BBC team on national TV, even though Hugh had moved
on, but this was the next best thing, going out to both the UK and
Europe. The only small drawback was that there was to be considerable
commuting back and forth from the event to the studios in Isleworth,
West London, all of two miles from my home.

The media have always been very well looked after at Badminton,
and on the Friday Whitbread held a lunch for the fourth estate. I was
sitting on a very lively table when we were joined by a considerably
refreshed and talkative Irishman, whom none of us regulars had met.
Lunch progressed and our new friend continued to refresh himself
liberally. Eventually he flaked out and was carted out feet first. A
minute later a smirking Hugh Thomas tapped me on the shoulder:
'You know who that was? He's your co-commentator tomorrow!' No
names, no pack drill, but he was on parade, right as rain, at 9.00am in
London the following morning.

The producer was trying to get us to hype it up a bit (very Sky) and
was suggesting we bill Leslie Law as the 'new Richard Meade', the only
British rider to have won individual Olympic gold. We resisted this
ridiculous notion. Of course, in 2004 Leslie Law became the second
British rider to win the individual Olympic gold!

We recorded a little package about the fences, which got me going,
then went live. It was an odd sensation commentating on something
happening over 100 miles (160km) away, but strangely a mixture of a
rider's adrenalin and the broadcasting made it an exhilarating first.

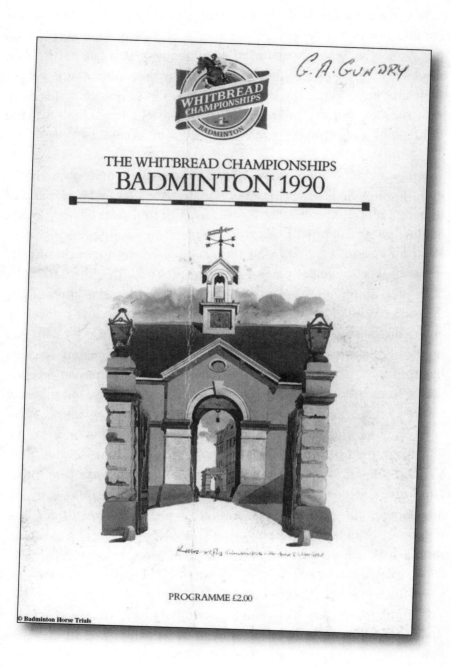

When we had finished it was back in haste down the M4 to meet my parents and fiancé Annabel for dinner at the Petty France. I arrived looking a bit of a mess, having had headphones on for five hours, been smoking in the small sound booth with my co-commentator for the same amount of time, and dashed back to Gloucestershire. A stiff drink was in order, but my mother sent me off to change. There was me thinking I had been quite grown up doing a bit of telly.

Twenty-six combinations show jumped clear, 10 of them inside the time, and 51 completed the event out of the 74 starters. Only 10 who started didn't get round. The dressage leader was a first time rider Claire Bowley, another protégé of Mark Phillips as a Range Rover Young Rider scholar. With Fair Share they had won the National Young Rider title in the spring at the Bramham Three Day Event in Yorkshire. She had had a taste of Badminton the year before, having ridden the 'guinea pig' dressage test, used to get the judges' eyes in before the first competitor enters the arena. In second place after this phase was a rider who had briefly been a lodger of mine when I lived in South Kensington. She had been up for a Christmas job at Harrods. Nicky McIrvine had recently parted from her successful event training husband Jonny, but much of his work on the horse Middle Road was in evidence during the weekend.

In eventing there are myriad opportunities for hard luck stories. We saw this next drama unfold on our monitor screens: New Zealand rider Vaughn Jefferis was having a fantastic round on his horse Enterprise. Unfortunately the chinstrap of his helmet came undone quite early on, breaching some subparagraph section of the rule book. Riders are notorious for not knowing every dotted 'I' or crossed 'T', but Vaughn should have known this one. He galloped on regardless until he was flagged down by an official with the end of the course in sight, and given the bad news of his elimination.

Coming into the show jumping, second last to go, Nicky and Middle Road jumped clear, with half a time fault. In came Claire Bowley and Fair Share, only one and a half points in the lead.

Poor Claire froze in the headlights, and Fair Share kicked down five fences and was just into time penalties too. Down to 12th they tumbled. Into second moved a future World Champion, Blyth Tait on Messiah for New Zealand, but there on top was Nicky McIrvine on Middle Road. She had made the best of her one-horse chance and retired not long after when the horse never really came back to form. She went on to marry Sebastian Coe.

If I gave the impression earlier that my form guide was pretty reliable, the following cost me several drinks among the press corps and a humble congratulatory letter to Nicky:

'Middle Road, Nicola McIrvine: They've done the trip before and were placed at Rotherfield last year. It's a strong field here so they will be lucky to make an impression at the very top.'

A new sponsor

The Championships in the autumn of 1990 were at Stockholm. The cross country course was in a municipal park right in the middle of the city. The British won the team silver, helped by a splendidly bravado-inspired round by Ian Stark and Murphy Himself, who bounced a wide road crossing where all sane combinations had put in a stride.

Ensconced with Derek 'Tommo' Thompson in our sound booth in Isleworth, it was hard not to utter an oath on air as they took this outrageous liberty and pulled it off. There had, however, been some dissent in the British camp. Throughout the history of eventing there have always been team competitions at Olympic, World and European Championships. These had been scored by adding the individual points together, in the old days counting all, but for a long time discarding the worst. Unlike a real equestrian team sport such as polo, however, eventing is an individual sport for 99 per cent of the time for

The Badminton Horse Trials
for the Mitsubishi Motors Trophy
May 7th–10th 1992

THE MITSUBISHI MOTORS TROPHY

Programme £2.00

99.9 per cent of the participants. The once-a-year challenge for the chosen four, (now five at the Olympics) requires a completely alien mind set. With team eventing, the chef d'equipe (manager) will issue team instructions. I prefer to call the team a squad, with a tactical plan.

Within the draw of teams, the manager can send riders in his preferred order. They will look for the first out to put a solid clear round in the bag, without thought of personal glory. The team rookie may well go next followed by the other good reliable banker. By this stage the competition will be fascinating to read. If the first three went clear, the final one to go, the one with the best chance of an individual medal, will be given carte blanche to go for it.

If one of the early ones has had a disaster, the last one must go safe and clear with no heroics. Also, rather more controversially, the manager can dictate which options the riders take at obstacles with a choice of routes. Sometimes this may just be the edict to take the longer but safer way. Sometimes, however, riders of bold horses actually feel safer going the direct route. It also doesn't greatly help the psyche to have your chosen route questioned.

Rodney Powell's The Irishman II had been fifth in 1987, thirteenth in 1988, third at Badminton in 1989 with Mark Todd on board and sixth with Rodney up again in 1990. He got his team call up for the Stockholm World Equestrian Games. He disobeyed team orders. He incurred 20 penalties. He became a non-person. Despite coming sixth individually and helping the squad's silver effort, Rodney was disillusioned with team riding. He would ride The Irishman at the next Badminton and put him on the market. With no Olympic ambition, Rodney reckoned that a good sale would set him up in a yard for life.

Leader after the dressage was Mary (Thomson) King, with King Boris just over five penalties ahead of consistent northern rider Helen Bell and Troubleshooter. David O'Connor and Wilton Fair were third for the USA, with Ian and Murphy fourth, happily close to the action.

Mary was fifth on her other ride, King William, and Rodney was handy in sixth.

On Saturday King Boris gave the crowd their money's worth by depositing Mary in The Lake. It wasn't her day, as King William slipped on the flat in Huntsman's Close, clocking up 60 penalties. Lorna Clarke pulled off one of her oft-repeated feats of pulling up from 30th to sixth overnight (and fourth eventually) with King's Jester. Rodney and The Irishman were the only combination inside the time, though they did get a small penalty on the steeplechase, and moved into second. Poor Ginny Leng had a rotten time on her swap-shop horse Griffin and retired, while Ian made it worse for her by storming into the lead with Murphy Himself. He hadn't, however, left himself a fence in hand. Rodney put on the pressure by going clear, one of only eight to do so, and Ian came into the arena. Hard to anchor after the exuberance of the cross country, all was fine until the ninth of 12 fences, when Murphy rolled it, to gift the title and the last ever Whitbread Trophy to Rodney and The Irishman II. That year the Princess of Wales came with the two young Princes to present the prizes.

Rodney did indeed sell the horse, to Bruce Davidson as a possible ride for the Barcelona Olympics. He went lame for a while and never got to the Games, but was used as a schoolmaster for Bruce's son Buck, before retiring. Rodney did rejoin the international squad some years later.

Whitbread had been a loyal sponsor since 1961, and its trophy one of the most recognised in sport, not least because of the longevity of their connection with Badminton. All good things must eventually come to an end, and even an event as famous as Badminton cannot assume that there will be queues of companies willing to invest a substantial amount of money over a period of time. As it turned out, a perfect partnership was formed in 1992 with a local, family owned, Cirencester business. No, Mr and Mrs Mitsubishi do not live in the Cotswolds. It was in fact The Colt Car Company which took on the sponsorship, as importers of the Mitsubishi brand. Though at first thought 'The Colt

Car Company Badminton Horse Trials' might have had a more equestrian ring to it, it was Mitsubishi cars the company was trying to promote. It was to be The Mitsubishi Motors Badminton Horse Trials. They signed up for three years to start with.

A new trophy was commissioned from local animal sculptress Judy Boyt, which, in an era of grossly tacky sporting silverware, was a shining example of clever design and impeccable taste. The basic concept was a tacked up, but unmounted, silver horse from each of the three disciplines. These would stand on a triangular base, incorporating the three joined diamonds of the Mitsubishi logo. The replicas for the placed riders would be of one of the horses, rotating annually round the disciplines. Presciently, one of the sculptures was based on King William.

Mitsubishi completely revamped the media centre, and it was run jointly by Jim Gilmore, who had been Badminton Press Officer since 1968, and Mitsubishi media man David Miles. They had both once worked on the same West Country newspaper.

As it happened they needed an experienced press team, with the best facilities, in that first year of Mitsubishi sponsorship. It was one of the rare 'incident years'. Despite the move to May, the English weather decided to play its unwelcome part again. It was cold, windy and wet, which always ups the stakes, and rendered the course more difficult than it might have been. The fastest round the cross country still got 13.6 time penalties, though 21 actually jumped round clear.

Mark Todd's Face the Music slipped going into the corner at fence 16 and caught his leg between the rails, breaking it. The horse was put down and the fence removed for the rest of the competition. (Riders who had already jumped it would have had time penalties adjusted.) Karen Lende and Mr Maxwell crashed into the ditch and bank at the Vicarage Vee, injuring the horse's spine, and he too had to be destroyed. Finally Susanna Macaire's Briarlands Pippin cartwheeled into The Lake with William Fox-Pitt, breaking the horse's back. None of these tragic accidents were particularly anyone's fault, but after incidents like this there is inevitably much soul searching.

After so many 'if only's' with King Boris, Mary triumphed with King William, taking home the trophy for which he had modelled. Ginny was second with Master Craftsman and yet another New Zealander, Vicky Latta, came third with Chief.

Lorna Clarke hung up her boots with an amazing 22 completions under her belt and went on to be a commentator with the BBC for many years afterwards.

On a lighter note, my very non-equestrian wife, of just over a year, said that last year's caravan experiment had not been a success. We duly booked into the Portcullis Inn at Tormarton. Mein Host admitted that he was something of a novice in the licensed victualer's trade. To say it was amateurishly run would besmirch amateurs. It was, however, pretty full. We had found some kindred spirits after supper and were having drinks in the snug when somebody walked up to the bar and took a swing at the publican. A great kerfuffle ensued. Turns out it was the ex-landlord. Hoping for similar sport we booked for the following year.

Soon after that I had been appointed PR for all three of the British Equestrian teams for the Barcelona Olympics, so found myself staying with the eventers at Badminton for their team concentration in July. We were all put up in the old servants' quarters, where the international riders stay during the event. It was weird, but very pleasant to be in the park with no tents or people, but there was inevitably excitement in the build up to the Games. Unfortunately the British team – Ian Stark on Murphy Himself, Mary Thomson (King) on King William, Richard Walker on Jacana and Karen Dixon on Get Smart – failed to win any medals at Barcelona.

Hot Toddy

Just as when a rider has a disappointing or disastrous event, and so wishes to have another go as soon as possible, it is surely the same with the executive when things have gone wrong. Sadly it is another year before you can bury the memory. Certainly Hugh Thomas took on board all the possible factors that might have caused the previous year's accidents. Course designers may have got away with certain forms of construction or presentation for many years, and it is only a mishap that will lead to a previously unthought-of way to keep the test the same, but the outcome safer, if a horse or rider makes a mistake. The ultimate safety of horse and rider are not only paramount, but must be seen to be so. The dilemma for the modern course designer is to combine safety with spectacle.

Much work was done on the take offs and landings to avoid slipping in wet years, and corner options were constructed either with a filled-in apex or strategic 'instant' trees to help riders avoid taking a dangerously impossible line. One or two have argued that this can take some responsibility away from the riders. Some international rules have also come in over the years, restricting, for example, the depth of the water in obstacles such as The Lake.

Everyone turned up at Badminton 1993 determined to have a 'good' event. There would be several new names, both human and equine, that would emerge near the top of the pile alongside familiar faces. Ginny had come with only Welton Houdini, who had fallen heavily the previous year at the rails by the Fairbanks Drop, and wasn't over confident about her chances. She had taken the horse hunting all season to get his confidence back. (She would marry Mikey Elliot, Field Master of the Heythrop, later that year.) They led the dressage by a whisker from Tanya Cleverly and Watkins. Mark Todd was third with Just an Ace, but faulted on the cross country, and also for New Zealand, Blyth Tait and Ricochet lay fifth behind France's Marie-Christine Duroy riding Quart du Placineau.

On the cross country 28 jumped clear, with 12 inside the time, which was a very satisfactory statistic to restore confidence all round. It was to Mitsubishi Motors' eternal credit that there had been no sharp intakes of breath when their first year of sponsorship did not go quite as they might have wished.

The hunting must have done its magic on Welton Houdini as he came into the show jumping on his dressage score and didn't add to it. Ginny had joined Mark Phillips in achieving a 'demi Lucinda' – three wins on three different horses. Tanya and Watkins had one down to drop to third, promoting Blyth to his second runner-up spot. Three other internationals were next, Vicky Latta and Chief (New Zealand), Anna Herman with Mr Punch (Sweden) and France's Marie-Christine Roy on Quart Du Placineau. A young William Fox-Pitt was next with Chaka and a future Burghley winner Charlotte Hollingsworth on The Cool Customer was eighth. Also in the money were two riders whose fathers had represented Great Britain in other sports. Bertie Blunt was ninth with Nick Burton on board. His father Mike played rugby for England and in 11th was McDuff III and Nicola Lewis, whose father was England cricket captain Peter May.

The Bevan family from Wales managed to reach the heights of both eventing and show jumping on a pretty tight budget. Ros was really the eventer and Lynne the jumper. Ros had won team junior European gold with Horton Venture in 1982 and then started out on Horton Point with considerable success. They had been fourth at Burghley and then ninth at Badminton in 1988. In 1989, however, the family lost their sponsor and went to extremes to keep the horse and an involvement in the sport. The most drastic move was to sell their house and live in a caravan!

On a more bizarre level though, they hatched a plan to sell a range of cuddly toys based on eventing characters. Sort of 'Badminton Bears'. Through Welsh family friend and Badminton commentator Justin Llewellyn (son of Bond film boffin 'Q', the late Desmond Llewellyn), they persuaded Lucinda, Toddy, Ginny, Ian and Frank Weldon to have alter ego bears. They also persuaded me to write the tags. You will understand that the intention was to remain anon:

VIRGINIA VOLE. Virginia Vole was a child star on the Riverbank. Her mother, named after the purple heather which covered the nearby heath, had planned it all. When she was a bit older she became friends with Toddy Teddy and in time they were to emerge as adult celebrities. Virginia also has a mutual friend with Scotie Dog, the grey, haired Irishman, Murphy. Apart from becoming the Vole Vaulting champion of the world, her Riverbank exploits have been well publicised because she looks good in her stage wardrobe. 'Roses are red and violets aren't blue, they're purple like I wear, and mother does too.'

Or

TODDY TEDDY. Unlike his neighbours the Koalas, who munch eucalyptus to relax, Toddy prefers sipping the juice of the kiwi fruits. As Teddies go, he is really quite slim and the nearest he's been to honey was dyeing his hair that colour once for a bet. Some years ago he put his worldly possessions into his black and white spotted hankie and crossed the world to seek fame and fortune. With the help of a few nips of Southern Comfort and his natural charisma, Toddy became a star, whilst still remaining unspoiled by stardom and very relaxed – perhaps he munches eucalyptus after all!

Despite all this, the Bevans were still afloat five years later, thanks to another family friend, Bob Rose, who set up a syndicate to help pay the bills. Ros had generously decided to pass the ride on to her younger sister Lynne, who as a show jumper, at least wasn't intimidated by the actual dimensions of the eventing fences.

Lynne completed Badminton three times with Horton Point and was ready to go in 1994 only to break her collarbone the weekend before. Mark Todd had trained Lynne a bit previously, and had liked the horse, so he was first choice as super sub. He was also riding Just an Ace, so would have an early and late draw. Horton Point was drawn number one. The Bevans admitted that they had never really gone full throttle on the cross country phase, not wishing to wear down the family pet, but knew that Toddy could safely squeak out a bit more speed.

It is funny how memories can play tricks, both to us spectators and riders, when being subsequently interviewed. Many of us recall it as the year that Mark and Sid went first, clear and inside the time, rendering the rest of the day an anticlimax, as they couldn't be beaten. Mark is also quoted in Debbie Sly's book as saying: 'I asked him for a little more pace towards the end of the course and he was able to respond. For the first time in his life he finished inside the time, which put him in the lead.' Well of course it did. He was first to go! Also, in theory he could have been beaten much later in the afternoon by Germany's Marina Loheit and Sundance Kid, who had led the dressage and were drawn number 57. The threat was real till the second Luckington Lane, where they fell.

Lynne missed Toddy's round on her pet, literally choking with emotion and a painkilling pill in the Red Cross tent. Yet another drama in the annals of the 10-minute box!

The Kiwis took four out of the first five places. Blyth was bridesmaid for the third time with Delta III and Vaughn Jefferis put his chinstrap disaster behind him to come third with Bounce. Separating the pack was America's Bruce Davidson with Eagle Lion, and Mark again was fifth with Just an Ace.

Horton Point retired after his triumph and Lynne went back to show jumping, winning the Queen Elizabeth Cup on a horse that Mark Todd had been having an unsuccessful show with at Hickstead in 1997.

I had now become officially part of the Badminton Media team.

David Miles, the Mitsubishi Press man, used to motor sport, suggested we had proper evening press conferences with the top three riders each day. My job was to ask some 'sensible' questions and then invite the floor to pose their own. This worked quite well in a light-hearted way, because most of the riders were friends of mine, and in theory I knew what I was talking about. I was also in a position to ask the occasional cheeky one. I would have my comeuppance another day.

Bruce's Badminton

American Bruce Davidson had been fourth in 1994 with Eagle Lion, a controversial third in 1974 with Irish Cap and second in 1982 with JJ Babu. He had also been a multiple medallist and twice World Champion, in 1974 at Burghley on Irish Cap, and Lexington four years later with Might Tango.

The big win, however, had always proved illusive. His 1995 campaign got off to a good start lying third after the dressage, behind leader William Fox-Pitt with his 1994 Burghley winner Chaka and former Individual Olympic gold medallist Matt Ryan from Australia on Kibah Tic Toc.

Out of an almost capacity 79 starters of the event, 31, more than a third, jumped clear, with nine inside the time. However, only 44 completed the event, only just over a half. It is this kind of statistic that confounds course designers. For the top half, the course would seem to have been too easy, and for the rest, too difficult.

On the Saturday my wife Annabel and I went to meet my parents at the Seafood Bar by the scoreboards. It had often been our rendezvous point, but over the years health and safety had decreed that only plastic cutlery and flutes were allowed, along with paper plates. Hardly in keeping with none too cheap lobster and bubbly. I did pass my comments on to Mr Thomas! However, that lunch proved very worth-while, as I spotted in the crowd Annabel's cousin Sarah Geoghegan, who I think I had only met once at her grandma's funeral. We had no idea she was a Badminton regular. We called her over and discovered she lived within walking distance of Gatcombe, and just down the road from where we were sitting. Ever since we have stayed with her for the event.

After the cross country William and Chaka were just two points ahead of Matt and Kibah Tic Toc, with Bruce less than four points behind Matt. The show jumping to come, was-as-ever, going to be crucial. Over the years clean sheets in this phase have been harder to come by than on the cross country.

Long before this jumping, however, all riders have to go through the final horse inspection. No-hopers don't bother to present. There is sometimes a heart-stopping moment when a horse is asked to re present. One or two are inevitably 'spun' or failed. The sensation of 1995 was that the overnight leader Chaka didn't pass. Of all the ways for dreams to be shattered.

There had been only two clear rounds in the morning session, and just five in the afternoon. One was from Mark Todd and Just an Ace, who rose to fourth; another was Karen O'Connor for the USA with Biko, up to third. Bruce was second last to go and went clear, leaving Matt to jump for the title. He had one down and half a time fault and had to settle for second.

Bruce had won at last and after the prize-giving and lap of honour he was scooped up by the media minders and brought to the press tent to be introduced to the waiting newshounds by your author, the novice Master of Ceremonies.

I may have been known by most of the riders, but had not apparently appeared on Bruce's radar. He answered each of my questions with a single syllable. I took my interviewing technique back to the drawing board.

Stark reality

In 1996 Hugh suggested that I might write Badminton-specific biographies of all the hundred-plus entered riders. That first year it was a mammoth undertaking as I was starting from scratch. It is still very time consuming when I do it now. I had to research their international records, Badminton history, and find out if by day they were rocket scientists or concert violinists. Over the years the event has indeed had a couple of airline pilots, a firewoman, a pop singer, a parfumier, a vet, a Naval Commander, an HGV driver, a former DHSS clerk, a chicken farmer and a psychoanalyst. (Not to mention a fashion designer!) Today the majority are usually full-time riders. The 'personal details' section, however, remains a bit of a minefield, as partners and spouses have been likely to change year by year, usually by name, but sometimes by gender.

One of the great heroics of 1995 had been Mark Todd's ride on Bertie Blunt. The horse had been ninth with his previous owner in 1993, Nick Burton. They had had an unhappy European Championships that year, when Nick, like Rodney some years before, had been accused of not playing for the team, by retiring from a fall. He put the horse on the market.

Riding Bertie at Burghley in the autumn of 1994, Mark was eliminated for missing a flag on the roads and tracks, though not informed until he had risked himself and the horse by riding into second place on the cross country. At the following Badminton all was going well until The Vicarage Pond, early on the course, when his left stirrup broke. He continued round 'one legged' to lie in fifth place overnight.

Sadly, Bertie Blunt joined Chaka to be among an unprecedented five who were spun on the Sunday morning.

Mark Todd actually lost the ride on Bertie Blunt between 1995 and 1996, having fallen out with one of his sponsors, but when the horse failed to sell, two of his other owners sent it back to him. After an early

The 1997
Mitsubishi
Motors
Badminton
Horse Trials

MITSUBISHI
MOTORS

May 8th - 11th
Programme £3
Save the Children

season win it was back to Badminton for another go. They did a good test to lie in third behind Ian Stark and Lady Hartington's Stanwick Ghost and at the top was America's David O'Connor on Custom Made. He was also fourth at this stage on Lightfoot. High wind during the first day of dressage played its part, with some combinations posting disappointing scores.

The new feature fence was at The Lake site, comprising a roofed jetty, requiring horse and rider to jump back into the water. Trailblazer Andrew Nicholson went clear inside the time on Cartoon, as did Mary King with King William, making up for their 27th place in the dressage, but several of the other early ones fell going the direct route at The Lake – at one stage two in a row, Eddie Stibbe and Bahlua and Terry Boon with Vulgan Nick. From then on most opted for the longer option as they found they could still do the time, literally going round the houses. Mary King, with her second horse Star Appeal clobbered the very first fence and fell off. She retired hurt and was too stiff to jump the next day.

Thirty-two jumped round clear, a quarter of them without time penalties. As it happens, Todd and Bertie Blunt and O'Connor with Custom Made incurred fractional ones which proved immaterial. The former retained his third position overnight, the latter dropped to second and Ian Stark stormed into the lead with Stanwick Ghost. Vaughn Jefferis moved up one, to fourth with Bounce and Leslie Law, on former Nicky Coe ride New Flavour, in fifth before the jumping.

On the Sunday the only placed combination not to present at the horse inspection was Mary King and King William. The three that failed the inspection were not in contention. Of the final ones into the arena, Blyth Tait went clear to secure fifth; Leslie with a quarter of a time fault, went up one to fourth. Both Vaughn and Mark were faultless, so the pressure was on the final two. Custom Made knocked one to go third, the spot his wife Karen had taken the previous year, but when Ian came into the ring he knew he had to go clear to win. He had two 'crowd groaners' on his way down to sixth, so the seemingly jinxed career of Bertie Blunt had been turned around as he emerged victorious.

I had been on the sport's media committee for some time, and for the past year had been holding the fort as employed PR for the then British Horse Trials Association (now British Eventing). I looked after the press, while Olympic rider Karen Dixon's husband Andrew handled the marketing. In yet another sporting cross-over, Andrew's father Robin Dixon (Lord Glentoran) had won a winter Olympic gold in the bobsleigh. We were searching for a candidate to take on the dual role permanently. We chose a sporting vicar's daughter, Juliette Brindley, who had had the distinction of driving at Le Mans.

For the second time I had been employed by the British Equestrian Federation to look after the media interests of our teams for the 1996 Atlanta Olympics. For the eventers, of course Badminton was the opportunity for riders to stake their claim. This year they had two bites of the selection cherry, as the Olympic authorities had decreed that there would be two competitions, one for individual medals and one for team. Needless to say this stirred up the debate as to which was the most prestigious, and who to select for what. (This ill-conceived format was repeated at Sydney in 2000.) Some countries were in the lucky position of having their top riders with two strings to their bow. They were therefore able to field seasoned Olympians in both contests. Certainly experience, both of team tactics (that seldom-needed mind set) and the completely different atmosphere of an Olympics was likely to pay dividends.

Jim Gilmore, the Badminton Press Officer, also found another very acceptable role for me. I was detailed to host a table in the inner sanctum of the director's tent for any of the Sports Editors of the national newspapers, and their families, who had accepted our invitation to a day out at the Trials. All of us involved with the event know that until someone has actually been, they have no concept of what a massive undertaking it is. Also the family aspect may be unrealised until witnessed.

Badminton has many similarities to its older sporting cousin, the Grand National, not least that almost every year a story emerges to remember that particular year by. I was learning that this certainly keeps the media centre on its toes.

The enormous, and impossible, entry of 151 for Badminton 1997 was an indication of several things in the sport. As reported earlier, in the Weldon era the idea of riders' rights would have been laughed at. The majority of his courses really did terrify those who turned up to try them, and certainly frightened many off coming in the first place. As the Colonel used to say: 'You don't have to come.'

With more people taking part in the sport generally, and more fancying their chances, tighter qualifications were necessary. The problem that this created, however, was that having had to try harder to qualify, once that had been achieved the rider felt entitled to have a run, whether actually up to it or not. This was a difficult one for the rule makers and is still with us today.

Also there had been concerted efforts to spread the sport to 'emerging' equestrian nations, not least to keep it in the Olympics. Though hotly disputed, some felt that the sport was in danger of dumbing down. If 151 people really thought they could tackle Badminton, was it still the challenge it had once been? One thing is certain. It had become a very different challenge. It was very different to the 'heart in mouth, shut eyes, kick and pray' days.

Technical riding skills were now at a premium over blind bravado. All courses were becoming, to use the jargon, 'more technical'. Of course all riders needed, and got, the nervous adrenalin as they were counted down, but they were now more worried about making silly mistakes rather than a visit to Bristol's Frenchay Hospital. Don't get me wrong. The sport, despite ever-continuing safety reviews, is still a challenge for the brave but now it is a challenge for the brave and more refined rider.

This vast entry was a precursor of things to come, but that first year caused organisational headaches. Hugh Thomas ended up between a rock and a hard place with his first solution to restrict overseas riders to one horse. The foreigners kicked up a heck of a fuss, and that old-fashioned feeling of it being a privilege to have a ride at Badminton was presented as a right to ride more than one. Not very edifying. The none too popular compromise was for the National Federations to fill their allotted slots how they wished to.

Now I was part of the Press team at Badminton, I used to attend the press lunch and drive round at the park, a few weeks before the event. In those days Mitsubishi had some small executive extravagances, which included a company helicopter. One of the treats that year was for some of us to be flown round the course, with the pilot 'jumping' us over The Lake and swooping over The Quarry. It was fantastic to see such a familiar place from such a different perspective. During the event, a past riding friend of mine, Duncan Douglas, enquired over a drink whether I had walked the course yet. 'Not exactly . . .'

After the slight unpleasantness in the build up, the competition got underway. Ian and Stanwick Ghost cruised round to lead after the two days from David O'Connor (one of the less agitated foreigners) for the USA and Custom Made. Mary King on Star Appeal made up for their blunder at the first the previous year and was lying third, with Andrew Hoy behind with Darien Powers. The latter didn't trot up on the last day.

A record 42 jumped round clear in the cross country with 16 making the time. This result was no doubt likely to encourage an equally big entry the following year, if the qualifications were to remain the same. Public sensitivities change however, and the sort of results that may have been acceptable in the 1960s and 1970s would no longer be tolerated. Also, of course, if half the field was to get eliminated early on round the course the paying public would have reason to feel short changed, having to wait for ages till the next horse came over the horizon.

A clear round in the jumping brought Blyth initially up from ninth to fifth, William Fox-Pitt and Cosmopolitan II from seventh to fourth. One fence down put Mary in third and David's quarter of a time fault guaranteed him one place higher than the year before.

For the second year running Ian and Stanwick Ghost were last into the arena to jump for the Mitsubishi Trophy. They knocked down no fewer than five to drop all the way out of the replica trophy winning top 12.

David had become the second American to win in three years and Star Appeal had earned his name back.

Golden oldie

People sometimes express surprise that I was doing my Badminton riding while I was a fashion student, understandably wondering how the two worlds could co-exist. There have, however, been some surprising overlaps.

In the 1980s I co-wrote a book on fashion illustration with a former fellow student. The publishers commissioned another. I was in Somerset at a party for equestrian photographer Kit Houghton's wife Kate, and was introduced to a very fashionable-looking guest, who was married to one of Kit's school friends. She was Wendy Dagworthy, a well-known designer from the 1970s, who was now head of my old college, Saint Martins. I had had nothing to do with the place for 20 years, but I suddenly thought that my second book could include work from the new era of top students. I arranged to see Wendy back in London and the book happened.

Quite separately, through my Badminton work filming with Alastair Martin-Bird and his co-producer Jamie Hawksfield, I was commissioned to write the script for the British Field Sports Society film on foxhunting. The director Richard Duplock came to see me at home, and after a couple of visits asked why I had fashion photos of girls in frocks on the wall. I explained that they were of my collection from my degree show.

Turned out Richard had done the same course as me eight years previously with all the same tutors. I think it goes without saying that the BFSS were unaware that they had two Saint Martins frock designers in charge of their award winning little film.

Later there were other coincidences. Both Mary Gordon-Watson and Pippa Funnell's brothers lived in different houses, within bread-roll-throwing distance from my abode in Gastein Road, London W6!

The outcome of various machinations found me teaching at Saint Martins from 1996, so fashion and eventing were my parallel universes again. This got even odder 10 years on when I recruited Harriet Worsley as an assistant lecturer for my Fashion Communication course. It transpired first that she was Alice (Plunkett) Fox-Pitt's best friend at school, but had also worked as PA to *Vogue* publisher Stephen Quinn. My sister Katie had been his PA at *Harpers and Queen*. The latter connection helped get me the job of writing the horsey bits for the Sloane Ranger Diary.

The spring of 1998 was looking very busy. I was teaching part time, organising fashion shoots on locations (sometimes sourced from event sites), writing the rider biographies, escorting students to Paris and Barcelona, contributing to the *Erotic Revue* and taping radio interviews with the great and the good for the Countryside March. For the latter I met John Mortimer, Peregrine Worsthorne, Lucinda Lambton, Ned Sherrin, Angela Rippon and Alan Lamb.

The night before the march, indefatigable fundraiser Rosemary Barlow had taken over Earls Court 2 in London for a cabaret and jolly. I was press ganged into organising one of the turns. I persuaded Ian Stark, Andrew Nicholson and Blyth Tait along with jump jockeys Chris Maude and Mick Fitzgerald to be The Village People.

Blyth was the cop, in breeches, boots, a leather jacket with no shirt, an old motorcycle helmet of mine and shades. Andrew was the Red

Indian in Speedos, chaps, lipsticked chest and my exotic feathered hat with fox's brushes each side. I found a chained leather cap in Kensington Market for Chris to set off his all black clobber, and since I knew him least, let Mick be the cowboy.

I think I forgot one of the ensemble, but the revelation of the evening was Ian as the construction worker. I provided a boiler suit and site helmet, and just told him to wear Timberland boots. He refused the boiler suit, however, producing a fetching pair of pink shorts and kept them on all night.

In the preceding few years the sport had endured several tragic accidents, which had unsurprisingly attracted a certain amount of press coverage. Those of us in the sport likely to have to deal with the media were sent on training courses, where we were interviewed on screen, asked difficult questions and generally advised on how to deal with enquiries. An entertaining chap called Hugo Brooke took several of these sessions. With a certain self-knowledge I asked him what I should do during a crisis if I was approached by a TV crew while I was wearing something a tad flamboyant. 'Julian, my boy, leg it.'

For my sins I had found myself elected in 1997 to the board of the British Horse Trials Association, the national governing body of eventing, so was coming to Badminton as one of the 'suits'.

The week of the event I got a rotten ear infection, which perforated my ear drums and rendered me as deaf as a post. This wasn't entirely helpful as on the Wednesday I had an audition with Meridian TV as a co-commentator with Tanya Cleverley for an eventing series they were doing. Rather generously they took my condition into account and I got the job. I still, however, had Badminton to deal with: rider interviews, radio etc.

Needless to say, sympathy from the press corps was negligible to the point of offence. Oh how they laughed as they mouthed at me silently.

British pride needed a boost at Badminton, as the last four winners had all been from overseas. So much for Badminton's historic roots, to get the home side up to speed and beat the foreigners. They had taken over. Was this going to happen again? When an unknown goes into the lead in the dressage, as Stuart Black and Market Venture did for Canada on the Friday, it tends to throw the press a bit. Trouble is that my biogs may not shed too much more light either, but then I can start the questions rolling at the press conference. Second equal was Mark Todd with Vicky Latta's Broadcast News and Owen Moore with Lightfoot. In fourth was the home side's best ever pure dressage rider Chris Bartle, with Word Perfect II, who had completed the previous year.

Some may find statistics a bit dry, but following them year by year just goes to show how one set of results can be so different to the next. The factors, of course, change: weather, class of field and the unknown element of how the course will ride.

A surprising 26 people got time faults on the steeplechase in 1998, though 32 jumped round the cross country clear, a 'better' result than the previous 42. Eleven were inside the time, a good number. Not a single horse fell, which is an excellent statistic, but riders parted company from their horses 13 times, which is also pretty acceptable.

By Saturday night Todd and Broadcast News, who had won the Open European Championships at Burghley the previous autumn, were in the lead at Badminton yet again. In second was Chris Bartle, only just over a point behind. The dressage leader Stuart Black went well enough to lie seventh. Bruce Davidson was up to fourth, Vaughn Jefferis fifth and Karen O'Connor sixth. Joining Bartle to defend Britain's honour was Tina Gifford and General Jock.

Since the early 1980s the trot ups had moved from the stable yard to the front of the house as they had become very well attended by spectators. This in turn had made them into something of a fashion parade, with the riders looking totally unrecognisable from their equestrian selves. That year the event's bespoke broadcaster, Radio Badminton, asked David O'Connor and me to judge proceedings as a beauty pageant on air. I'm not convinced I endeared myself to the mildly feminist producer, by describing one skirt-suited lady rider as looking like an airline 'trolley dolly'.

In the afternoon Tina had one down to finish sixth, Karen moved up to fifth, Vaughn and Bruce went clear for fourth and third respectively and then Chris came into the ring. An earlier rider, Charlotte Ridley, had suffered that rare lapse of memory and was eliminated for taking the wrong course. For one awful moment it looked as if Chris was going to do something similar, as Bertie Hill had done many years earlier when lying in the money. An audible intake of breath from the crowd woke Chris out of his reverie, and he jumped a clear round.

Then in came the overnight leader, Mark Todd and Broadcast News, reigning Open European Champions. For the third time Mark heard that sickening knock on wood that would cruelly take the title from under his nose. It had been the fourth year running that Badminton had been 'lost' not 'won'. No one really wants that type of ending after all the heroics of the week, but if nothing else it keeps the paying customers on the edges of their seats till the final second of four days of competition.

At 46 Chris had at that stage become the oldest person to win Badminton, beating Bill Roycroft by four days.

Happy anniversary

1999 heralded the 50th anniversary of 'Badminton'. And it was to be quite an event. There were to be several areas of controversy throughout.

From the start the weather was foul. Andrew Nicholson was disconcerted during his first test on Merillion to hear Sally O'Connor's headphone commentary coming out over the PA stating: 'Oh dear, a little stiff in the shoulder, he'll be marked down for that.' Andrew also took issue with one judge, Richard Meade, about his marks though Richard marked him top on his second horse New York. Andrew nevertheless sought 'clarification' and was reprimanded for his pains.

The FEI (International Equestrian Federation), of which Hugh Thomas just happened to be the chairman of its eventing committee, had revamped the scoring system, both for the dressage and the cross country timing where a penalty was given for every second over the time.

The course at Badminton is always strung on both sides along the 'fairway', and the position of the string has an enormous influence on the approach to the obstacles. The riders, who statistically had benefited from a couple of relatively benign Badmintons, were not slow in voicing their discontent. Ian Stark remarked: 'You need a cross between a gymkhana pony and a Grade A show jumper.' This witticism did, to a degree, forecast the way the sport was heading. So too did this advent of rider power.

The new system made the dressage scores higher than in the past, though this was led by Mark Todd on Broadcast News. Pippa Funnell did a good test to finish in second after that phase, but the dressage was swiftly to become an irrelevance.

On the Saturday two fences were removed: a big and quite narrow Hayrack away from Tom Smith's Walls and a post and rail into Huntsman's Close. Nevertheless there was all sorts of trouble out there. Only 10 made the time on the steeplechase, 19 went clear cross country but none anywhere near the time. With the new system there were enormous gaps between the scores.

Five were eliminated on the cross country, 24 retired. Two retired on the chase and five after the roads and tracks. Another five fell by the wayside at other points during the weekend. The most talked about event, however, was Australian Stuart Tinney's departure into the crowd. His horse Tex spotted a sight line on leaving The Lake and leaped over the spectator fence, narrowly missing the Disabled pen. They bowled over American cameraman, Melvin Cox, who was briefly hospitalised. Sportingly he was back the next day, arm in a sling.

After the rigours of the Saturday there were 31 left to jump, 11 of which had been first timers. Some new faces were up for a prize. Heidi Antikatzides for Greece came 10th with Michaelmas, Jeanette Brakewell and Over to You started what would be a long run, coming ninth. Pippa Funnell was sixth with Supreme Rock, young Austin O'Connor for Ireland had the ride of his life to be fourth on Simply Rhett and America's Kerry Millikin put two disastrous Badmintons behind her to be third. Eleventh and fifth was Andrew Nicholson on New York and Merillion, despite his complaints, and he was starting his assault on Lorna Clarke's record 22 finishes. All the top four had one show jump down but Mark was four fences adrift from Ian Stark on Lady Hartington's eight-year-old Jaybee so that the Stanwick Ghost could be put to rest.

Having had four consecutive years when the finale was a cliffhanger, the new system didn't really work. With a master spin, Hugh Thomas explained before the show jumping: 'Of course there's a huge gap, but I hope that rather than a nail-biting finish today will bring glorious displays of horsemanship and I think that is what everyone will come to watch.'

The 1999 result proved just how difficult it is to frame a competition such as Badminton. The weather played its part. The new scoring system proved wanting, but on a very positive note some first timers didn't whinge, put their heads down, got on with it and in several cases stated their case for a long and successful career in the sport. As Ian Stark said to Austin O'Connor: 'Oh to be so young,' to which Austin replied: 'And stupid.'

Being the 50th anniversary, Badminton welcomed Her Majesty the Queen for the first time in many years to present the prizes. Ian's win for the future Duchess of Devonshire was very popular with the home crowd, and there was a carriage drive round showing off many past winners of the great event.

Certainly the anniversary Badminton showed how far the event, and indeed the sport, had come since the 10th Duke had suggested his park as a venue. Now it was heading for the new millennium.

Star Appeal

In millennium year there were no fewer than 92 starters, which once again drew comment in the equestrian press about the level of qualifications needed to try for the ultimate challenge in the sport.

The early spring weather had not been promising, but by the time the riders congregated at Badminton in May the sun and wind had done their stuff. Cancellation would have been a PR disaster for Mitsubishi, as they were using Badminton to launch their new Shogun, and the loss of the most prestigious event can play havoc with international qualifications. A year out also hits the trade stand holders very hard. Badminton is often their biggest show of the year and coming at the beginning of their summer season on the road can have a serious impact on their entire year.

The set dressage test had reverted to the slightly easier 25-year-old version, as it was to be used in the two contests, individual and team, at the Sydney Olympics. The scoring system went back to normal after the unsatisfactory experiment of the year before.

The first day leader was another 'unknown', Tristram Owers and Hatherden's Riverdance, who was as surprised to be summoned to the media centre as were the journalists who had to interview him. The following day, however, the scribes were in their comfort zone when Andrew Hoy eased into the lead with Darien Powers. Second for France was Rodolphe Scherer with Bambi de Briere, with Leslie Law third on his second string, Matt Butler.

On cross country day the first to go were Gary Parsonage and Magic Rogue, who fell on the steeplechase and retired. Later in the day, on the figure of eight course Karen Dixon, let out of the traps too early, had to apply the brakes to avoid a scissors crash with Canadian rider Wyndham St John. Her few time penalties were rescinded on appeal.

It fell to Leslie Law and Shear H2O, who were eliminated the previous year, to venture out first on to the cross country. There were

29 obstacles on the course this time, and Leslie cleared them all, to come inside the time of just under 12½ minutes. Both the number of fences and distances had reduced gradually from the 1970s, and the endurance phase was shortened too, in line with FEI safety recommendations. These modifications should not be seen, however, as making the test necessarily easier, because horses were being asked to make roughly the same number of jumping efforts in a shorter space, arguably making the test just as stiff. As ever for course designers, getting the balance was a never-ending conundrum.

With this more compact course, and the fact that for TV purposes the start and finish of cross country day had to fit the 'live' schedules, the vast entry were sent off at three-minute intervals, instead of the usual four. This would have kept the officials at 'air traffic control' on their toes, but would certainly have given the spectators a full afternoon's entertainment. Thirty-three jumped clear, with seven inside the time, which for Hugh must have been a gratifying statistic.

Two previous winners had an unhappy weekend. William retired Stunning at the Vicarage Vee and Moon Man stopped one from home, while Chris Bartle had a fall at the new Beer Garden mushroom, which also sent Tina Gifford to Frenchay Hospital, with Oscar and had a stop with Word Perfect at fence 19. The Beer Garden also tripped up Eddie Stibbe and Century Fox along with Katie Parker and Springleaze Macaroo, and sent Heidi Antikatzides to Frenchay as well.

The oft-repeated mantra that horses are great levellers was repeated during the afternoon, when other big names totted up the penalties. Blyth Tait and Chesterfield came too strongly to the Pheasant Feeders at six and fell; Andrew Hoy, the dressage leader with Darien Powers, had a 'silly' run out at the Bullfinch after the ditch at the Shogun Sport Turn. Andrew Nicholson and Whitmonday also faulted here, though he stormed round on New York.

First day leader Tristram Owers had a great ride to finish 17th on Saturday evening, only to plummet to 42nd on Sunday with 55 penalties in the jumping. Other first timers fared better. Caroline Pratt

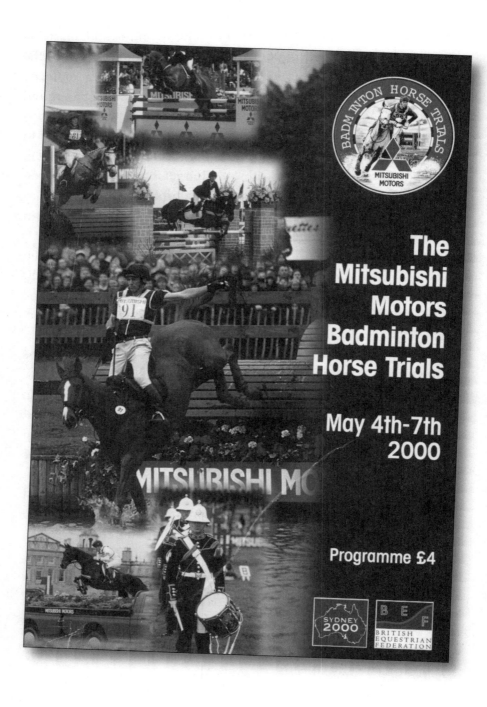

pulled up to 12th overnight with Primitive Control and Caroline Powell, who had formerly groomed for Ian Stark, found herself in the limelight with Dalliance. Paul O'Brien, based with Blyth for many years, stepped out of the shadow of his mentor and had a great round on Enzed. Brook Staples and Master Monarch lay ninth overnight.

Coming into the show jumping, there were several British combinations forming a line of resistance against an Antipodean onslaught: Louisa Lockwood with Fair Impression, Karen Dixon on The Honourable Bob, Caroline Pratt with Primitive Control, Rodney Powell riding Flintstone, Leslie on the pathfinder Shear H2O, and in the lead, Mary King and Star Appeal.

The final top 12 were: Lockwood 12th, Powell (NZ) 11th, O'Brien (NZ) 10th, Hoy (AUS) ninth, Nicholson (NZ) eighth, Ryan (AUS) seventh, Pratt sixth, Todd (NZ) fifth, Staples (AUS) fourth, Powell third, Law second, and jumping clear to take the title again, Mary King, whose long time faith in Star Appeal had been vindicated.

A mammoth 59 took home the Portcullis plaques for completing the event. One of these was Alice Plunkett, now one of the faces of Channel 4 Racing (and Mrs William Fox-Pitt). As she was coming to the end of the cross country, I received a call over my walkie-talkie, rather interrupting my smart lunch in the Director's Tent. Could I please get down to the finish pronto, for a possible interview with Alice by Clare Balding. This was a bittersweet moment.

When I had eventually completed Aintree 12 years previously, I seriously thought I would be the last of an exclusive little club of about half a dozen, who had competed and completed the Badminton/Liverpool double. Alice, like Chris Collins before us, had done her racing first, and here she was about to get round the big event. It was a very good excuse to take her out to dinner later in the year.

Fantasy Badminton

The season of 2001 was over before it had started. The outbreak of foot and mouth disease had put paid to most country sports, and the decision to abandon Badminton was taken very early. That strangely made the disappointment easier to absorb. Riders had longer to make alternative qualification plans, and traders might just have known in time not to carry too much stock for the year.

The equestrian magazines were also a bit stuck about what to put in their editions. Actually, both editors and writers had to be a bit more inventive, so we had some fun. In what would have been the Badminton preview edition, *Horse & Hound* asked me to write a 'Fantasy Badminton' piece. It was the good old chestnut along the lines of: 'Who was the greatest of them all?' For a bit of fun and as something knowledgeable readers can dispute, this was it:

FANTASY BADMINTON
It should have been Badminton next week but don't despair – we've found an alternative to set you thinking. Julian Seaman fed the form of the 'greats' into a computer to see what might have happened if Frank Weldon and Mark Todd had competed head to head. The results may not be what you'd expected. . . .

It has always been hard to predict the winners of a real Badminton, particularly in the certain knowledge that one would offend those not tipped and put the traditional curse on those one did. Now I have been set the truly impossible task of attempting to do a 'greatest of all time' in the spirit of 'Would Ali have beaten Tyson?', 'If Arkle had run in the Grand National, would he have beaten Red Rum?' or 'Was Fangio greater than Schumacher?' Incongruously, Red Rum won the National but Lucinda won Badminton. In this spirit, I have started with the riders, although I have taken their horses into account too. Sometimes a horse and rider combination has set the world alight, sometimes a brilliant rider has found a tune from a mediocre horse or a chance ride – there are so many variables to feed into the fantasy computer, and the fun part is that absolutely no one will agree with my result.

By definition, I have looked at their form at the time they won, who they beat and by how much (trying to find a middle way through the changing scoring systems), rather than how it compares today.

The variables: First the course. The dimensions for horse trials fences were set as long ago as 1912, before Badminton was thought of, so the jumps today are no bigger or wider. The timber has become more imposing over the years, although this has made the fences more inviting. The endurance part used to be longer and included until quite recently, a 5min steeplechase. One could also make up for a poor dressage by gaining bonus points on the cross country.

From 1960 to 1965, the event was split into 'Great' and 'Little' Badminton sections, the latter always being regarded as the lesser. The event used to be run in April, so the going was heavier and there were fewer One Day Events in which to acquire skills. 'Frank's rider frighteners' in late 1960s and 1970s certainly did; no one had seen anything like his fences before. Not that Col. Weldon was infallible, but I don't think anyone dared suggest he might have erred.

Until relatively recently, fences were much more 'country natural', which often meant less well defined ground lines, and there was an era of the spectator-thrilling but jarring big drop fences. Hairy, but fabulous to ride when it went well. When the event moved to May in 1988 the going became faster, but by now the senior riders were beyond the 'shut your eyes and kick' horror of the old days and needed something a bit technical to sort them out. The fences have become more difficult, but because of the increasing expertise in design and the fantastic presentation by the Willis brothers, some of the margins for rider error have been taken away. For example, at the Vicarage Vee, a rider today cannot try an impossible corner, but is guided to the long or short route by the 'unjumpable bit'.

The X-Factor: Most riders today are much better at dressage than their forbears. It would be true to say that the Badminton pioneers agreed with this passage in Col. Hope's *The Horse Trials Story*: 'The prevalent notion of the continental horseman was someone who spent his time bumming around the arena teasing his horse.'

Despite the fact that a few eventers have show jumped at top level, this remains an Achilles' heel and so often the competition is lost on the last day. Show jumping at a One Day Event just cannot prepare horse and rider for the same test after the rigours of Badminton Saturday. In the old days a knockdown cost twice as much as it does today. Given the task of creating a top 10 from the whole history of Badminton, it was impossible to overload the list with more recent contenders, so some recent stars haven't made the cut – sorry Ian and Mary.

All the contenders in Fantasy Badminton have won the ultimate eventing prize. The courses have changed, the rules have changed, the date has changed, but who is the greatest of the great?

And the nominees are:

Bill Roycroft 1960. Forty-one years ago the Antipodean spirit, which has resurfaced to such an incredible effect now, was shown when the Australian squad came over on a slow boat en route to the Rome Olympics, working their horses on deck. Bill Roycroft, 46, won Badminton on the 15hh Our Solo, while his team mate Laurie Morgan came second. They went on to take team gold. Bill shares with Lorna Clarke the now unachievable feat of completing Badminton on three horses in a single year. Winning margin 3.6; 20 starters.

Frank Weldon 1955, 1956. Forged a great partnership with probably the first classic event horse, Kilbarry, and scored one of his wins in 1955 when Badminton hosted the European Championships and was, confusingly, held at Windsor. One of the subsequent former CO's of the King's Troop to play a big part in the sport, Frank came into his own as the autocratic course designer and director. Unlike most of his generation he seemed to have got the hang of the dressage bit. Not convinced he would have liked to ride the scariest courses he set for others. Today's funny angles might have caught them out. Best winning margin 41.78; 53 starters (1955).

John Shedden 1949. The Yuri Gagarin of the Badminton experience. Winning the first running, wearing hunting kit to ride cross country, he and Golden Willow won by a margin of 26.5. John was runner up the following year with Kingpin. He deserves his place in history, having gone into the unknown and won it in some style, but anything a bit technical could have presented a problem. Went into space, but was never destined to go to the moon. Winning margin 26.5; 22 starters.

Mark Todd 1980, 1994, 1996. What looked like a fluke in 1980 on Southern Comfort at his first attempt heralded the arrival of one of the all-time eventing greats. The double Olympic Champion won on the chance ride Horton Point and again on Bertie Blunt. He has also show jumped at Olympic level. A class act. Best winning margin 12.4; 80 starters (1994).

Mark Phillips 1971, 1972, 1974, 1981. The first to overtake Sheila Willcox's three wins, Mark has since had conspicuous success as a trainer and course designer. He got the best results on the least good of his rides. Unlucky on perhaps his best horse Persian Holiday, he triumphed with Great Ovation, the runaway Columbus and the not that inspiring Lincoln. Had show jumped at high level so had the accuracy to ride the technical courses he now sets for other people. Best winning margin 30.2; 48 starters (1971).

Anneli Drummond-Hay 1962. Riding Merely a Monarch, Anneli had already won the inaugural Burghley the previous autumn by more than 33 points. They could actually do dressage, which was a considerable help, and had the best score in all three phases. A film charting their attempt in 1962 was the inspiration for this scribe, and they won it by a margin of 42. The duo went on to achieve top level success in show jumping and Anneli was still jumping in international championships for South Africa in the 1990s. Winning margin 42; 19 starters.

Lucinda Green 1973, 1976, 1977, 1979, 1983, 1984. Six wins, six horses, Queen of eventing's golden era, her record speaks for itself and I doubt it will ever be bettered. Be Fair, the Pony Club ride; Wideawake, who dramatically keeled over at the prize-giving; Elaine Straker's George; the honest but one-paced Killaire; the flashy Regal Realm and finally Beagle Bay. An inspiration to a generation of aspiring riders, who today has some interestingly controversial ideas as to where the sport might progress. Best winning margin 28.65; 48 starters (1977).

Ginny Elliot 1985, 1989, 1993. The former junior champion had a fallow period and nearly lost an arm in a fall before having a truly purple patch. Did eventing PR a vast amount of good by being a genuinely photogenic winner. Unbeatable at her peak, she had some super horses, selected by her mother Heather and trained by Dot Willis. Best winning margin 3.6; 58 starters (1989).

Sheila Willcox 1957, 1958, 1959. The sport's first 'faux' professional, Sheila took this emerging discipline to new heights. Her dedication and single-mindedness paid off. One of the purists, Sheila knew the park well and would find all the shortest routes. Very competitive. Mary King was a pupil. Best winning margin 47; 58 starters (1958).

Richard Meade 1970, 1982. Britain's individual Olympic gold medallist, Richard so nearly won Badminton in 1972 as well, but for time faults in the show jumping. He was unofficial team captain when owners were expected to lay down their horses for their country, with R Meade to pilot – not an altogether unsuccessful approach. With wins spanning 12 years, he stands the test of time. Best wining margin 4.4; 46 starters (1970).

And the Winner is . . .

1st Anneli Drummond-Hay. She could do dressage, she can show jump and she seemed able to tackle anything then, so although the fences have changed, I bet she could still do it now. Who knows what might have happened had Merely a Monarch's talent not taken the show jumping route after their Badminton win?

2nd Lucinda Green. It almost surprises me not to put her at the top. Very close call.

3rd Mark Todd. If you were the owner of a four-star horse and you wanted the reflected glory of a win at that level, he would be your man.

4th Sheila Willcox. The first multiple winner on more than one horse, and probably the first eventing specialist.

5th Mark Phillips. Had an amazing ability to get a tune out of unpromising material.

6th Ginny Elliot. Was excellent at bringing on horses from the start and the best PR news for eventing during the style-conscious 1980s.

7th Frank Weldon. It was there before him and flourishes today, but Frank put his mark on the course like no other.

8th Richard Meade. A field master with the Beaufort, he made the best of the cherry picking days and his wins, 12 years apart, stood the test of time.

9th Bill Roycroft. The spirit of 1960 obviously lives on and the 'feisty stockman' approach seems to be paying dividends these days. Australian eventing is on a high.

10th John Shedden. Wouldn't be among the leaders today but he paved the way for all the others to follow. Won the first running and came second on a different horse next time out.

2001 was to have been Jim Gilmore's swansong as Press Officer after 35 years and in his eighties. The Duke held a party for him in Badminton House in the autumn to say thank you, and without the benefit of a year as understudy your author stepped into some very big shoes.

PART 5

MEDIA MAN (2002–PRESENT)

The office

I had known that I was going to be the new Press Officer from the summer of 2000 and had already been to have a meeting with David Miles at Mitsubishi. I had been involved in the press tent for many years and was familiar with how the operation worked during the event, but Jim with his enormous experience was very kind, first for endorsing my pitch for the job, but also giving me great encouragement and advice.

There is probably a little something I do for Badminton nearly every day of the year, but obviously from January to the event in May it builds up to a crescendo. Since I have had the job, I get several calls and emails each year from keen graduates asking to do work experience in the office that runs the Media operation. They probably note the London address and make some assumptions. My nerve centre rather resembles that of Badminton's first director, Trevor Horn, only my filing rests on an upright piano, not a baby grand!

When the competition is in full swing there is an army of helpers and professionals, including fence judges, stewards, vets and doctors and also contractors and services such as the police. The actual 'home team' however, is remarkably small for what is a world famous event. The main office is occupied by the director, Hugh Thomas, Assistant Director Jane Tuckwell, admin managers Sue Ansell and Willa Harford, and in the build up Carole Alexander at the Box Office. This number is boosted in the closing build up by one or two more in and about the office, including Harry Verney, the site manager, and his team. The increasingly busy Willis family, the course designers, are out in the park turning Hugh's imagination into reality. In the run up to the event I have two days when my wife, and recently a friend Peter de Cosimo, who used to manage Chris Bartle's Yorkshire Riding Establishment, stuff envelopes and when a demon typing expert, Sally Reilly, comes to make sense of my 150 rider biogs. My empire is in Fulham, west London.

The job is very much in two distinctive parts. Before the event I will write probably three or four press releases, one to go out in early January basically reminding the world that Badminton preparations are underway. The next one will be when all the entries are in, and finally one to coincide with our press day a couple of weeks before the Trials, describing the new course. There may well be an extra one if we have something like a new BBC deal to announce.

Prospective journalists must apply on our website to be considered for accreditation. It comes to about 300 journalists and 200 photographers. There is a set day in April when accreditation closes. I will have been down to the office at Badminton to pick up all the car passes and letters of instructions for the media, and we have the aforementioned mailing day. Jim Gilmore showed me a brilliant low-tech system for cross referencing when I get the inevitable calls saying that so and so has not got their passes.

It is so simple, it is brilliant. Each car pass is numbered at the printers. I buy an address book. As we stuff an envelope I write the recipient's name on their alphabetical address book page, noting whether they are a photographer or journalist, how many are coming in on the one car pass and logging the pass number. When they ring, as some surely do to blag an extra pass, I can quote the number. I have had the occasional innocent, claiming that they had the bumph but not the badge – 99 per cent impossible with my system. (Won't tempt providence by claiming 100 per cent.) When I suggest they look down by their feet, lo and behold they had dropped it out of the envelope.

For four months the phone calls and the emails are non-stop. I also organise the guest list for our press lunch, a meeting with the BBC and other TV companies, tee up radio interviews, and pass on TV rights enquiries to our agents. I will probably do one or two media interviews myself, but prefer to put Hugh or a rider up.

The press day has an eclectic cast. Representatives from the national press and equestrian press are joined by local publications. Badminton is that rare thing, an extravaganza of international importance, which is nevertheless a very local event. There will also be one or two radio stations. (We have a separate TV day.) Everyone turns up at 10.30am, has coffee in the Main Hall, and greeted by Hugh. We then set off round the course in a fleet of Mitsubishis, stopping off at some of the new obstacles. One of the great and good of the national press (all good friends!) habitually calls me the day before and says; 'When I am late Julian, please send a car over to pick me up.' 'How about leaving just a bit earlier?'

After the drive round, it is back to the hall for a drink, when we are joined by the Duke and Duchess and go through for lunch. In the early years a bit of a scrum for seats then ensued, and on the suggestion from the Duchess, I now do a fixed table plan, which works much better.

By the time I get to the event on the Tuesday, part one of the job is done. There are always late accreditations, sometimes justified if an agency scribe or snapper has suddenly been given the gig, but others need to do some horrible pleading even to be considered.

Having enjoyed the facilities of the media centre for several years, I have become a bit of a poacher turned gamekeeper, but I do like my tent to have a welcoming atmosphere, for those who are meant to be in there! I have a team of three indispensable helpers, Becky, Emma and Paul, who works for British Eventing, all of whom are very experienced and can call up riders for interviews, dispense photographers' tabards and field enquiries. I also have a full-time journalist, Carole Mortimer, who creates about 30 rolling stories during the week. Kit Houghton, who is Badminton's official photographer, takes charge of his colleagues.

The media sign in with my team each day. The tent has two areas, one social with a bar, tables and food, the other with work stations, an interview stage and photographers' zone. Both areas have a three-feed bank of TV screens, so on cross country day the media should see all of the action. I relinquished my interviewing role to Peter Morris, a legally trained Cirencester Agricultural College lecturer. It is universally accepted that he does a much better job than I ever did. Delegation, that's the future.

Over the years I have slept in all sorts of places during the Trials. Caravan in the competitors' park, Petty France Hotel, amateur pub, and even a couple of times in the public caravan park. I must say that in a year of decent weather as a family outing for a few days, the latter seemed really the best. One thousand sites are now allocated and another 300 for the hardy tent dwellers.

Having discovered Annabel's cousin Sarah near Tetbury, we stay there as a family. My son Freddie was two the first year I was Press Officer. Now I have a well-tried weekly routine. On Tuesday and Wednesday I stay with Sarah, and depending on whether I go to the cocktail party or not, either return on the Thursday, or kip in a caravan I have insisted on having tucked in behind the media centre. (They always start off by parking it by the loos, generators, or both!) This is essentially for Friday night, when I cannot afford to be anywhere off site. For supper on Friday I now usually go armed with a bottle of wine and join the British Eventing gang in their caravan.

My stays at Badminton for the Olympic build ups helped me plan on site mornings. I drive in my courtesy Mitsubishi to the back of the house, make my way up to the half dozen bathrooms in the old servants' quarters, armed with shaving gear and hair dryer, and come back down to the fantastic, antler-festooned servants' hall to join all the grooms at the trestle tables for a full English breakfast. I come back via the picturesque village shop, once featured in a Miss Marple episode, to pick up all the daily papers. I am at my desk by eight.

There is naturally happy anticipation for the competition after a year of abandonment, and though Hugh had no doubt had a radical course change in his mind before the foot and mouth outbreak, 2002 was when it was unveiled. The old traditional start, pointing houseward, and hanging either left or right on alternate years was now in the main arena, which also contained the first and last jumps. Badminton's relatively flat topography nevertheless has some natural features which have played host to the designers' creations. The cluster zones of famous obstacles would elicit comment each year as to what Frank or

Hugh had done with The Quarry, The Lake or Huntsman's Close. Would Tom Smith's Walls be in this year? What jumps would criss-cross the Vicarage Ditch?

Hugh would continue to utilise many of these zones, but with the start in a different place, the dynamic of the course, which had become familiar in either direction, would necessarily change enormously. The route would need to alter too since The Lake, which for many years had been the halfway point, would have been a far too early fence three on a right-handed start. To the disappointment of some traditionalists, the new layout seemed to preclude the use of the Luckington Lane and the famous fences the other side of it.

Reigning European Champion Pippa Funnell, going second last of the 87 starters, went into the lead in the dressage by six points with Supreme Rock, from Andrew Hoy with Darien Powers, and Rodney Powell, on the Boucher's Flintstone in third.

Hugh's course proved to ride as technically as it looked, bringing back memories of Ian Stark's assessment that a Grade A show jumping gymkhana pony was needed. 'Rocky' was neither of these. Thirty-eight jumped clear, but only four made the time, including Andrew Hoy and Andrew Nicholson on New York. Also clear inside the time was William Fox-Pitt with his new big hope, Mary, and Finn Guinness's Tamarillo. This was a great feat by William as he was suffering from acute groin strain, so much so that he didn't start his second ride Moon Man. Pippa got 5.2 time penalties, minimising her lead.

Every year the event gets more and more international. Brazil's first Badminton entry, Guto de Faria and Hunefer, under the expert guidance of Tiny Clapham, who since our Pony Club days had won a team silver at Los Angeles, had a great debut round as did Germany's Andres Dibowski and Ginger, who finished fourth. Another happy rider was Kate Lambie, from New Zealand, who risked all by selling her other horses and brought over her home winning mare Nufarm Alibi. She finished fifth, top of the Kiwis ahead of Nicholson's two rides and Heelan Tompkins. There were six nations in the top 10. Germany,

Greece (Heidi Antikatzides, trained by Brynley Powell), New Zealand, Australia (Hoy), USA (Amy Tryon, the firefighter) and three Britons.

Flintstone and Rodney Powell were eliminated on the cross country, but Leslie Law finished Saturday fifth and William third. Hoy lying second had a disastrous four show jumps down (now only worth four penalties) to slip to eighth. Law moved to third. William went clear and Pippa had a fence in hand. She kept the poles up, got one time penalty and won by a margin of four. It had been a British one-two-three, but a united nations down the line. Pippa had become the first to lead from the front since Ginny in 1993.

Flying the course

Badminton had been shown live on the BBC since 1954, but this year it clashed with the FA Cup Final and was only going to be shown as a package on the Sunday, going as live to the final show jumping rounds. This caused considerable consternation to armchair fans, but there are two viewpoints. An edited programme can have more relevance to a non-equestrian audience, and do away with the producer's nightmare of having a long delay while going live. It does require an overnight edit, however. Hugh believes, on the other hand, that the risk is worth taking to get a BBC1 Saturday audience, as opposed to a shorter slot on BBC2 on Sunday. With the advent of digital TV the keenest are able to watch every round on 'red button'. A few delays wouldn't matter to them. The general TV public can see a shorter live slot or a package.

Jim had sometimes put me forward to do some local TV interviews during the event, which were always quite fun. The year that my son Freddie was born, Annabel stayed away from Badminton so I escorted cousin Sarah. I was doing a couple of pieces with Chris Searle, one of the old *That's Life* team, when one of the production staff came up to us and said: 'I think you are being stalked by a fan.' Turned out to be Sarah.

In 2002 however I was going to go national. The BBC *Six O'Clock News* was going to go 'live' to Badminton. There had been some worry that the FA Cup Final, being played at the Millennium Stadium in Cardiff, would cause havoc with the M4 traffic. I had recorded some preliminary bits and was standing on spot X among the trade stands ready to be counted in. I was lined up looking at the camera waiting for the first question, when the director signalled a cut throat. The veteran Labour politician Barbara Castle had shuffled off this mortal coil, and was dominating the news. A nation was spared. As it turned out, the football traffic and the event traffic never clashed.

I had been lucky that my first year as Press Officer had taken place during a year of little media drama at the event, and I was very grateful for the amount of goodwill and advice that came my way. My flirtations with TV, making Badminton videos, commentating for Eurosport, and helping to produce several local eventing series for Meridian made me very interested in the BBC operation at Badminton. The long-time producing husband and wife team of Jonny Watherstone and Wendy Shepherd had recently retired and the new director, Chris Lewis, sometimes indulged one or two of my suggestions. The previous year at our TV meeting I had mooted an alternative way of showing the jumps in the preview package.

Many years ago for the Grand National they had flown a helicopter round the course with a low-slung camera. The pilot 'jumped' the fences and it gave a very passable sensation of being there. With the advent of minicams they put them in jockeys' helmets. Without getting too technical, the head wobble in the early minicams with insufficient gyroscopes gave a very unconvincing view. A rider's head may go up and down with the rhythm, but the sight line stays fixed.

For Badminton, unlike Aintree, it would be unthinkable at present to send a stunt cameraman round the course for a preview. For a start, a horse and rider combination capable of doing the job would almost certainly be a competitor, and also the ground could get dug up. (Way back in history the previous Duke did test out some of the jumps on one of his hunters.)

My two joy rides round Badminton in the Mitsubishi helicopter were a great experience, but I could see that there was no way of getting close enough for a decent TV shot, unlike a racecourse.

My thoughts went back to making the foxhunting film with my Saint Martins' director friend Richard Duplock. He had been hired for that job on the strength of several 'How To' films on fishing and shooting. He had told me he had once used a camera mounted in a remote control model helicopter, to fly with the birds. I had once talked the idea up with Meridian, but it had come to nothing. This could be just the thing for Badminton. In 2002 it was a bit close to the event to, as one might say, get the idea off the ground, but at the equivalent meeting in 2003 Chris and Hugh agreed to fund my whim 50/50.

I had been warned by Richard that the 'pilot' and cameraman were a bit eccentric, which perhaps is not surprising in adults who fly 'toys' for a living. I duly booked them for the Tuesday of the event. We were at the mercy of the weather, because even a moderate breeze can cancel the shoot. Insurance against this was so astronomical that we took the risk.

On the Monday I called to make a rendezvous. 'Oh sorry mate, hasn't the girl at the BBC told you? We can't come, I've done my back.' I only needed him to fly a blooming toy helicopter. 'I won't be able to lift it out of the truck.' 'Look chum, I can provide the muscle, you get here with your mate and your machine.' By a great coincidence I had told Sue (Hatherley) Benson of my plans at the press day, and she had revealed that her strapping student son was greatly into model aeroplane flying. At an instant we had a thoroughly engaged assistant.

The homemade machine was actually rather bigger than I had imagined, about 3ft (1m) long, but it was great to watch. Okay, I admit it, I love model planes too, so I was in nerdy heaven. I could direct the shots from a monitor in their truck, choosing the routes the riders might take. The one guy flies the chopper, the other wiggles his joysticks to move the camera. It was great because we could really do it from a rider's eye view, up and over, and down the drops, with no wobble. The little stunt had worked.

In my first year fronting the tent I had David Miles of Mitsubishi to help me along, and Jim, bless him, hovering with the best of intentions. Mitsubishi have an enormous role in the setting up and running of the technical side of the centre, providing IT support and many other services, such as providing cars and drivers. Their team also sits alongside mine at the front desk. Over the years we have built up a strong relationship. David had left the company after the 2002 event, so I was keen to meet his replacement Gabi Whitfield. She was working for Nissan in Paris. 'No Julian, you can wait till the press day', said Hugh, rather unsportingly.

The sponsor's hospitality marquee had always been the far side of the trade stand village from the media centre. Now they were side by side with a communal catering facility. This brought event and sponsor close both geographically and psychologically. The event office is also yards away.

The very top level of the sport had a new valuable carrot to dangle at the riders. Rolex, the sponsors of the Lexington Three Day Event, which usually takes place the week before Badminton, put up a prize of $250,000 for any rider who could win all of the three top events, Badminton, Burghley and Lexington, in a row. The first prize for Badminton in 2003 was £37,500. This presupposed that the top riders had more than one international level horse, but this had been the norm for some time. Although the challenge was well nigh impossible, it opened up the prospect of any one of the three events hosting a nail biter. The week before Badminton Pippa Funnell had won Lexington by the smallest margin from Polly Stockton, finishing on the same score but winning on differentials. When she arrived in

Gloucestershire with her reigning champion Supreme Rock it was 'game on' for the accumulator.

The morning of the Thursday was wet and very blustery, with much of the tentage flapping loudly. Andrew Nicholson and Mr Smiffy went in fourth and coped well with the conditions to do a test that would keep him in a handy sixth place after both dressage days, and Pippa, going 10th on her second string, Cornerman, settled in seventh. Late on Thursday, first timer Piia Pantsu from Finland, who had only ever seen footage of Badminton, performed a polished test to take a first day lead and a final dressage spot in third on Ypaja Karuso. Slightly controversially, Lucinda Fredericks did a presentable test on Darasass to go =12th then promptly announced that she was withdrawing because she was four months' pregnant. These days, when the entry list is likely to be oversubscribed, starting with no intention of doing more than a dressage school may not be seen as playing the game.

Most of the better tests were on the Friday. William Fox-Pitt and Tamarillo, number 100, slipped into fifth, Andrew Hoy and Moon Fleet (93) went fourth and Germany's Bettina Hoy, Andrew's wife, lay second with Ringwood Cockatoo. Just over one point better though was the defending champion, Pippa Funnell with Supreme Rock.

Tamarillo was withdrawn on Saturday morning with a bit of heat in a leg, leaving 74 combinations to take on what looked to be a challenging cross country course, made more so by the dreadful weather. The first element of the 23rd obstacle, The Shogun Field Hollow, was removed. This was the rail before the ditch to the rail away. Another fence that was causing much discussion was the Carisma Puzzle, right at the far end of the Vicarage Ditch at the Wiltshire part of the course. The first element of either option was a gaping ditch. The right-hand option was a bounce to an upright brush, affording more space to the 'out', the left, a stride, but a bounce to a very narrow section of brush.

As it turned out, this fence caused quite a bit of trouble. Bettina put herself out of contention there. Clayton Fredericks flew through the air when Absolute Novelty stopped abruptly and Karen Dixon dislocated her shoulder there, falling from Uptotrix. The crowd got their money's worth at The Lake. There were seven tip-ups there, including Clayton, for his second flying display of the day, this time from On Patrol, and the Riding Master of the Household Cavalry, Richard Waygood and Master Fred. The only real casualty here was Sweden's Anna Hasso, whose ride decanted her in the water, then fell on top of her, breaking her pelvis. Happily she made a full recovery. The others were first timer Rhian Smith with Bush Powder, Neil Fox (Young Thomas), Dan Jocelyn (Silence) and Sweden's Anna Hilton, parting company with Limerick Star, even after going the long route after a stop. The oldest horse in the competition, 17-year-old Barclay Square, retired at The Lake despite completing the previous year, and the oldest rider, the veteran Bruce Davidson, fell twice with Apparition, ending up in hospital with a shoulder injury.

There was to be controversy late in the afternoon. Just after 4.00pm, when 53 horses had cleared the Carisma Puzzle, officials removed the fence for safety reasons. The landing side of the bank had become slippery, but the stone dust put down to give more grip gave an optical illusion to the groundline. There were only 12 more combinations to go, mostly the most experienced on their second rides. Scores were rejigged, but these decisions are never popular. Jeanette Brakewell and Over to You had been third, but demoted to fifth with the revised scores. Honour was eventually satisfied on Sunday when her clear show jumping brought her back to finish third, and she would never have beaten the top two. Piia Pantsu, the penultimate to go with Ypaja Karuso, jumped clear to retain second on a score of 44.4. Pippa, on 34, had two fences in hand. Then she knocked one. Proceeding with perhaps just a tad too much caution, she cleared all the jumps, but the clock was ticking. To the gasps of the crowd, she picked up six time penalties . . . and won her second Badminton in a row by point four of a penalty. As she told the assembled media at the press conference: 'All my connections will be pleased that I made some improvement on my winning margin in Kentucky!'

Pippa had now won two legs of the Rolex Challenge, by point four penalties, in two weeks of competition. In a great boost for the concept, Pippa went on to achieve the impossible at Burghley in the autumn.

Family ties

There have been some families with more than one Badminton competitor to celebrate. The most obvious are the spouses, not least because they will have met through a love of the sport. Then there are the siblings, then the rare couple who have bred a Badminton rider. So far the latter category can only, I think, claim Oliver and Marietta Fox-Pitt, Polly and Hamish Lochore and Princess Anne and Mark for producing William, Alec and Zara.

Husband and wife combos go back to Viv and George Boon in the 1950s, Val and Bill Henson and with the Fox- Pitt and Lochore seniors in the 1960s, Angela and Mike Tucker in the 1970s, with Mark and Princess Anne, followed by Hugh Thomas and his first wife Anne and Lucinda and David Green. Then come Mark Phillips and his second wife Sandy, Mandy and Eddie Stibbe, Bettina and Andrew Hoy with finally Clea and Vere Phillips and Phillip and Rosie Clapham.

With the siblings there is usually one ahead of the other, though both Drummond-Hay sisters were right up there, but Anneli won it and Jane's best was second. With the Martin-Birds, Angela was second once, with Tessa 13th that year and her best 9th. The Welsh Brookes sisters were about equal. Helen Butler, Anne Thomas' sister, had some good rides and was placed on Merganser; Mike Bullen set the pace, but it was little sister Jane who won it twice. Nigel Taylor had more rides, but Anne Marie has a better international record.

There have been a few times where siblings have turned up and either retired, withdrew or were eliminated. They can remain anonymous. The Bevan sisters were both placed on the same horse, which then won it for them with Mark Todd riding, and then there are the Strakers and Claphams, who fielded three. Matt and his brother Nick completed, but little sister Karen became the multiple Olympian. The Claphams older sister Tiny got Olympic silver, but both Sue and Phillip competed.

After all this time I can only find records of 14 children following their parents round, though this might increase in the future. Perhaps all parents were sufficiently scared not to wish the experience on their little darlings. Honours are about equal. Some of the parents fared better, and some of the children went one up.

Douglas (1950s) and Caroline Darling (1970s) would be about level. Bill Roycroft (1960s) would have it over Clarke (1970s); Bridget's Olympic gold would trump Katie Parker's consistent rounds. William easily is the Fox-Pitt star, whereas Bertie Hill (1960s) has a better and longer record than Tony (1970s). If you average out Polly and Hamish Lochore (1970s), Alec (1990s) would be about the same; similarly Guy and Julian Wathen (1960s to 1970s). There have also been Tony and Angela Buhler, Bill and Alfie Buller and Hans and Alfred Schwarzenbach. Lucy Wiegersma well outshines father Hendrick, but though Harry Meade has an enormous act to follow, he yet might do it one day. So far Princess Anne's Badminton record is better than Zara's, but whereas the Princess was European Champion, silver medallist and Olympian, Zara has been European and World Champion.

After the success of the toy helicopter shots we thought we would have another go at Badminton. It wasn't a gimmick we would use forever, but a couple of times seemed a good idea. I got hold of the company and repeated the booking.

This time there was no whinging about bad backs, but the typical wind-sucking pessimism of an itinerant plumber when they arrived on site. 'Ooh, it's a bit windy.' Well it was just a little bit more so than the previous year. They took ages to prime the machine, cannibalising some bits from their spare bit of kit. At last they were airborne and filming a drop fence early on the course. The first decent four-second shot took over an hour to get in the can. I know filming takes time, but this was very tedious.

Eventually the head man suggested that we get the most important jump done, then see what time and light we had left. Off we went to The Lake. The assistant producer Gabby Cook and I told the chap the shot we wanted and went to sit in the truck, to watch on the monitor. There was a fence into the water, one actually in the lake and a bank out to a narrow 'skinny' brush. His first take was pretty good. He came in, hopped it over the jump in the water, over the bank and out. The only trouble was that not a single rider would have taken his approach. 'Take 2 please maestro.'

'We never like to go again when we have one in the bag.'

'Yes but we can't use that one. Another go please.'

Very grudgingly they took off again. Gabby and I were happy with the approach. It was good in the water, up over the bank . . . 'Gabby he looks verrrrry close to the jump Flaaaaag . . . Smash, bang, wallop, one totalled model helicopter. Great shot (unusable) and a very upset operator. Thank goodness he had his spare machine. It took forever to prime it and get it in the air, but in the end we got our shots. They probably wouldn't have come again even if I had wanted them to.

It made for an eventful start to what would be a very busy week. With what turned out to be 13 TV crews descending, my team and I had our work cut out. TV crews always need a minder so one of us was out and about almost constantly during the event. We had two Eurosport documentary crews making programmes about Pippa and William (with more luck than the crews from years ago) a gang from Athens, local BBC, local ITV, news teams, BBC local business, all sorts.

The week may have started a bit too blustery for the model helicopter, but it just got worse and worse for horses and spectators as the competition unfolded. It was dark and windy when the Thursday dressage session started, and the very first to go, Caroline Pratt, had a dreadful time with Primitive Control, as he reared and lunged his way through the test to achieve the wooden spoon when the other 79 starters had completed the phase on Friday afternoon. First day leader was Megan Jones from Australia, who had sold several horses at home to pay for her trip over in a bid to impress her selectors.

Most of the best tests were on the second day, with Matthew Wright and Mallards Treat going fourth equal with Andrew Hoy and Mr Pracatan. Second equal were Pippa Funnel and Cornerman and William Fox-Pitt, still champing to win his first Badminton. He had been second on Tamarillo two years before, and was unable to jump when in the lead with Chaka. The only trouble was that the deep going was not at all ideal. 'He was bred to go in the desert', William bemoaned.

Top of the tree, however, was Andrew Nicholson and the Salmon's Lord Killinghurst. Andrew was setting off for his 21st and 22nd completion, fast catching up Lorna Clarke's record of 22. A win, though, would have been his greater ambition.

On cross country day William was in two minds whether to run, but he needed to qualify for Athens and the alternative strategy wasn't satisfactory. It didn't help that his first ride on Moon Man had ended with a stop three from home at The Quarry.

Pippa too had a beastly time, being catapulted out of the saddle from Viceroy jumping the gate going to Huntsman's Close. She then got trodden on and airlifted to the hospital for a check up. She was whisked back to the event by her mother after a tetanus jab, and set off on the roads and tracks with her second go with Cornerman. All went well until the same jump, where Cornerman made the same mistake as Viceroy and deposited the reigning dual champion on the deck for the second time that day. Poor Tina Cook fell off one from home with Captain Christie when he turned a bit too sharply at the Rolex fence.

The going was such that nobody got anywhere near the optimum time. The fastest was Kate Wood from New Zealand with just 15.6

time penalties, but hampered by a 74th dressage placing. Next fastest was British prospect Sarah Cutteridge and The Wexford Lady with 16.8 followed by part-time vet James Robinson and Comanche with 17.6. That put them in good stead for the final day. Bumble Thomas, who had faulted the previous year had a great round to lie fourth on Sunday morning.

Overnight the dressage placings had reversed for the top two, Fox-Pitt and Nicholson, the fiercest of opponents for myriad reasons. The heavy going had taken its toll, and five didn't trot up and one was spun at the final horse inspection.

There were only six clear jumping rounds of the 50 that tried and only nine had one down. Andrew Hoy had three down to go from third to fifth, the next three had two, with Nicholson also notching up a couple of time penalties. William, who had fortuitously decided to have a go cross country, cantered into the arena with a little bit of a cushion. He needed it, as he too rolled a couple, but emerged a deserving winner of the Mitsubishi Trophy.

In the summer I had a bit of a treat. My father had owned a four in hand, Park Drag coach since before I was born, bought for a song while at Sandhurst. He had been a member of the Coaching Club for some years and the club organised various drives during the year. A former Duke of Beaufort had been President of the Coaching Club and the current Duke invited the club to a meet at Badminton in August. A good dozen coaches assembled and we went for a wonderful drive round the estate and came back for dinner in the historic servants' hall. All sorts of people find themselves at Badminton. Two of the guests on that occasion were TV people Rolf Harris and Esther Rantzen. It was very special to be on the coach I had known all my life (first outing to old Tweseldown aged two), driving round Badminton Park, another life-long involvement.

As explained right at the beginning of this journey through the history of the event, the format that had evolved from all sorts of exotic computations had settled into the following familiar pattern of: dressage, spread if needed over two days; speed, endurance and cross country day, comprising phase A roads and tracks, four to five minute steeplechase, phase C roads and tracks, 10-minute break and 12- to 15-minute 30+ fence cross country; final day show jumping in reverse order of placings. There had been many modifications, too technical to go into here (penalty zones, dressage coefficients, phase E, minimum weights, banned substances and scoring tweaks). All of these had a subtle effect as the sport progressed. However, the international governing body was about to implement a change that would alter the very nature of Three Day Eventing. Under the guise of making the sport more inclusive to the emerging equestrian nations (I admire the euphemism), and thus retaining Olympic status, the endurance phases of roads and tracks and steeplechase would hence be abandoned for Olympic, World and Continental championships. This wasn't a tweak but a radical change to the whole concept of the sport. Three Day Events would now effectively be One Day Events run over three days. There was a logic to the idea which was unsurprisingly endorsed by emerging nations. In practical terms, a much smaller acreage would be needed to run a Three Day Event so more places could run them.

Many traditionalists were aghast. Would riders bother to get their horses fit enough? Would the favoured thoroughbred make way for the heavier warm bloods? Would this make it a glorified dressage competition? How could riders and horses tackle a four-star course without the limber up of the roads and tracks and steeplechase? How indeed would they warm up?

There was a great deal of consulting between the top three events, Badminton, Burghley and Lexington. There has always been an unspoken acknowledgement that while national grant-awarding bodies and the international federation consider the Championships the sport's pinnacle, the reality is that the top independent four-stars (Burghley and Badminton) are a greater test, (even in graded star level).

There was now a dilemma. What would be the point of retaining what was termed 'long format' if all the Championships and their qualifiers were 'short'? There was some discussion that the big ones could retain 'long' and market themselves as Classics. However, riders might have expected an even higher prize pot effectively just to be able to run their top rides twice a year. With 'short' they could run much more often.

Hugh was seriously considering going 'short' in 2005 and 'lead the field'. Some expressed a worry that the event's position as the world leader could be compromised if Lexington and Burghley didn't 'go short'. No disgrace in being last man down, they counselled. The big three agreed to stay 'long' for 2005 to let the experiment be tested at lesser events, with the hope of some that the traditional format could be retained for the showcase events. Sadly this turned out to be Canute-like optimism, and everyone knew by the spring of that year that we were about to see the end of an era.

Short format

Before the build up to the 2005 event the decision had been made that from 2006 the short format would be the one. Rather strangely the long one still exists in some outposts, for events at much lower levels. Considering that the long format Three Day Event was the ultimate test, retaining it at lower levels seems a bit odd, even for the 'stick in mud' romantics who regret its passing.

Badminton and Burghley put out a joint release. This is the gist:

WORLD'S TOP TWO HORSE TRIALS TO EMBRACE NEW CROSS COUNTRY FORMAT FROM 2006.
British Eventing's proposal for the world's most famous Horse Trials, Badminton and Burghley, to adopt the modified cross

country format from 2006 has been agreed by both Events, after over a year of consultation and worldwide trials. BE chairman Michael Tucker said: 'Last year we wanted to take time to evaluate the implications of the International changes of removing the roads and tracks and steeplechase phases, and after much debate the new format has emerged as the preferred way for the sport at present. We feel it is right to adopt the Olympic, World and European template to give our riders the best chance of medals in the future.'

He continued: 'The production of horses to the level of skill required to compete at Badminton and Burghley takes years. Riders, trainers and organisers need time to plan ahead for what some see as a radical development, which is why we have to make decisions now for next year. It is for this reason that Badminton and Burghley made a deliberate decision to retain the existing format in 2005 while the new arrangement settles down at lesser Events.'

Director of the Mitsubishi Motors Badminton Horse Trials, Hugh Thomas added: 'Our Trials were of course instigated as an Olympic preparation, and the sport of eventing, as the consummate test of all round horsemanship, has been seen in many guises since it was introduced at the Stockholm Olympics in 1912. The gradual fine tuning of the shape of the competition requires evolution, but not revolution. At Badminton from 2006 we will provide the fair but ultimate challenge in our sport, and as ever a fine spectacle for our visitors.'

Liz Inman, the incoming Director of The Land Rover Burghley Horse Trials said; 'These are the two greatest Events in the world at the highest possible level. By embracing the formula now in place for the International Championships, Burghley and Badminton will continue to be the benchmark for Events throughout our sport. Through the many Championships we have hosted, the site and organisation at Burghley has proved that it has the capacity to accommodate different types of competition with ease. We are looking forward to the challenge of presenting this new format in 2006 with positive and open minds.'

I won't pretend. It was hard to have part written the above, but we had one more long format to go, and then see how the new look would work out in 2006.

Perhaps a bit disappointingly, Hugh had broken with tradition and not reversed the route of the course this time. It gave the appearance of only having a few new obstacles, but beware any rider who assumes that what looks the same as the previous year is the identical fence. The Tote had a presence at Badminton again. They had Pippa's Primore's Pride and William's Tamarillo as joint favourites at 8/1.

Having kept quiet about clever ideas for the BBC for a year, I put another proposition to BBC director Chris Lewis. Over the years the headcams had become much less 'wobble vision'. Our toy helicopter shots had been great for the preview, but of course showed no crowds or action. As a rider, the unique experience of Badminton is riding into the vast crowd at The Lake. To say it is intimidating is an understatement. I thought that for the highlights programme it would be great to have a shot of this. They do it live from the Grand National, but there they don't record it as we would have to do, they beam it to the TV helicopter. Badminton did, for several years, have a chopper in the sky for the whole of Saturday, but to be frank the noise was a big downer on the entertainment factor. The National only lasts 10 minutes.

The producer Michael Cole went with the idea and said he would hire in the cameras. With the hindsight of the previous film crew experiences, we thought we'd get about half a dozen riders wired up, to ensure we got some usable footage. I got on the phone and recruited seven game jockeys.

I usually spend cross country day in my tent, watching every move on the three-screen close circuit TV screens. I see most of what is going on. I always station one of my team in the start and finish box. This time it was Winnie Murphy, then PR for the sport, who apart from her usual task of ushering the riders to interviews, was this time going to assist with kitting them up with the camera packs. She was ideal in that role as all the riders knew her.

It is easy to say this now, but I thought that though the helmet camera looked very neat, the recorder in a bum bag looked a bit cumbersome. I had wrongly assumed they had been used for this purpose before. We were all to discover the difference between down-hill skiing and riding cross country. My first volunteer was Polly Jackson on Limestone Rise. I watched with some consternation as I saw the bum bag come loose and swing by Polly's side. She had a stop at a fence, which may or may not have been due to the recorder bag, but it can't have helped. I rang Winnie and instantly cancelled all other camera trips. It is a measure of the help I get that Winnie had quite rightly already made her own executive decision. Not till the recorders are the size of a slim mobile phone will we try that again. In fact they probably do exist by now, so I might have another go one day.

One of the star columnists who nearly always covers Badminton is Simon Barnes of *The Times*. As it happens, he is a mustard-keen amateur rider himself. His paper started doing charity auctions for readers, to bid for a family day out with their favourite *Times* journalist. For example, seeing a play with their theatre critic, or a tour of the Stock Exchange with their economics editor. Top bid that year was a day with Simon Barnes at Badminton. Could I help?

Actually Simon and I managed to do a bit more than a day, hopefully achieving one of those 'money can't buy' experiences. Well I suppose money did buy it, but for a good cause! We did stable visits, a course drive, VIP seats and an autograph opportunity at the press conference. We might have spoilt it by presenting the family our latest books. They came to look us up again the following year, when they came as 'civilians' (as celebs refer to non-celebs in tabloid terms).

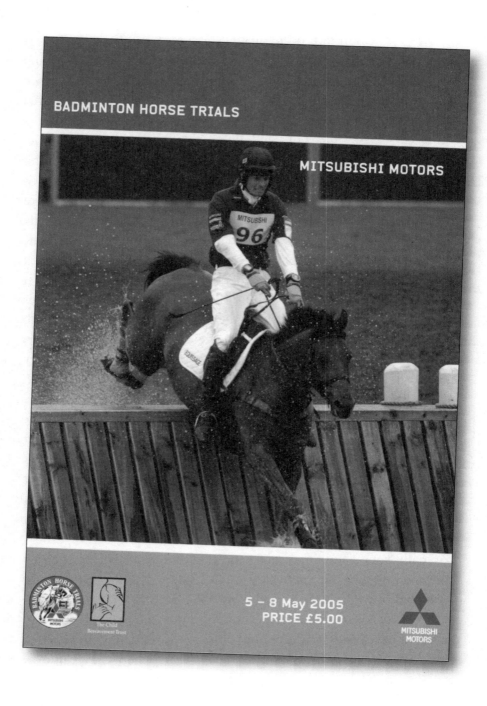

I don't always have time to get to the cocktail party, but this year there were no pressing crises to keep us in the tent, and for the first time the Mitsubishi media team were able to come along too. I familiarised them with 'Seaman's Patent Cocktail Party Manoeuvre', and escorted them to the do. As we were leaving, Gabi turned to me, suitably impressed and exclaimed: 'It works!'

Pippa and William were at the top of their game. William was the defending champion and Pippa had won the two previous runnings. Any unlikely complacency in her camp would have had a reality check with their duff Badminton in 2004. Primmore's Pride had won Kentucky and also been the horse to take Burghley and secure the Rolex purse. Both horses were day two dressage performers. Pippa went a couple before William and issued the challenge by going into the lead. William couldn't quite match it but went into second, only 5.2 behind.

The cross country produced 10 more clears this year than the last, over the similar track, posting 40 without jumping penalties and 11 inside the time. At the end of the Saturday, however, a new crowd favourite had emerged into third place, ahead of his mentor Andrew Hoy, and just behind the two main protagonists.

Yoshiaki Oiwa, Badminton's first ever Japanese competitor, had excited the crowds, the Mitsubishi sponsors and his country's Ambassador, to storm round the course like an old pro with Voyou du Roc, smiling as he went. Andrew, behind him in fourth, was riding Master Monarch, who in an ownership dispute, had at one stage been 'horsenapped' in daylight from the Hoy yard (at Princess Anne's Gatcombe Park, of all places) by his former rider, Australia's Brooke Staples and his partner, Jeanette Brakewell. All very Dick Francis.

Fifth overnight was Andrew Nicholson and Lord Killinghurst, who were about to complete for the 23rd time and overtake Lorna Clarke's record.

Sadly, Yoshi had three show jumps down to drop to 11th, but the other seven top contenders went clear, leaving Pippa to win again with a nerve-wrackingly tight margin of 1.6 from William.

Rolling back the years

After each event I usually write up my media report for Hugh the next day, while my on-the-spot notes still mean something. There is always a bit of an empty feeling after something as big as Badminton, however it has gone, whether you are a rider or any part of the set up as a whole. There is still a lot to do. For some years I would wait a few weeks to let Hugh tie up all his ends (and he starts thinking of the next year almost straight away), then arrange to go down to Badminton and have a pub lunch to go through my observations.

In 2006 we thought it might be fun to ring the changes. Hugh was coming up to London to have an Olympic meeting with Seb Coe, so I suggested we might meet at my rather disreputable haunt, The Chelsea Arts Club. Hugh understandably arrived wearing a suit, fresh from his meeting, to discover the somewhat exotic membership rather more louchely attired. We go there every year now, as Hugh sees it as his annual fix of Bohemia, and nearly dresses accordingly.

In what was seen as a welcome indication of remaining for longer as title sponsor, Mitsubishi decided on some re-branding. This included new signage, typeface and a new logo. Since their takeover there had been two images. The first was a flat chestnut jumping through the three red diamond Mitsubishi icon. Next was an all action, full colour, nearly photographic image of a grey horse, head on, splashing through a water jump, with a slightly un-Badminton hilly backdrop. Aesthetically it was good, but had one serious flaw which had not occurred to the designer. It was a very recognisable image of David Green. Nothing against D. Green, but in a sport as relatively small as eventing, a more 'everyman' image might have been more appropriate.

The new logo had to be designed to work on a small scale, on for example compliment slips, or for big flags and banners. The 'Green' version was even woven into a floor rug. When David, who always used to come and clear the media centre out of used notepads at the end of the event, heard that a new logo was in the offing, he asked Hugh whether he might possibly have the carpet. It had become the doormat at the Trials office in Badminton village.

Hugh turned down Greenie's request, with the teasing answer that it was too satisfying to wipe his feet on David's image each day.

Hugh, Jane and I were at a routine meeting in Cirencester with Mitsubishi when at the end they produced some prototypes for us to have a quick glance at. To be honest we didn't pay too much attention, as there would be another opportunity. Later though, Hugh called me and said he had reservations about the design. Although the image had been sourced from a Badminton action shot and 'graphiqued', it didn't convey the 'Badminton' essence. Could I have a crack at it?

It was quite a testing commission, as I was not to start from scratch, since much of the design style had been approved; indeed, I, too, liked it. What was wrong, rather crucially, was the image. The brief was: 'Jumping up, left to right, in a circle, suitable for black and white and a version with green and red livery.'

I took inspiration from a drawing by equestrian artist Joan Wanklyn, who had drawn several of the early Badminton programme covers. It was a wonderfully extravagant leap, based possibly on John Smart riding J.P.L.L. Esq., but not obviously so. I sifted through hundreds of photos, scanned some into my computer and started playing around. Eventually I found just the one, but it was going right to left. No problem to flip it round. Happily it was approved, and satisfying honour all round, went back to the Mitsubishi corporate studio for final conversion ready for 2006.

Though the debate about the format change had rumbled through the previous two years, the die was cast and everyone was assembled for the new look Badminton. It should be recognised that although the subject had exercised active equestrian enthusiasts, for the vast number of spectators it would make no difference whatsoever. Only the early birds used to watch the steeplechase efforts of the first riders, and no one ventured on to the roads and tracks unless they had arrived and erroneously marched off on phase A. Once, when I was riding, I did in fact come across a lost family, way out of the park, and directed them back to the action.

Unusually there was a bit of controversy on the first day of dressage. After British Open Champion Ruth Edge had gone into the lead with Two Thyme, ahead of Terry Boone on his 2004 Bramham winner Foreign Exchange, William Fox-Pitt did an adequate, but not brilliant, test on the mercurial Tamarillo, to lie in a perfectly respectable sixth on the first day with 49.8. Rumours abounded that William was going to pull out, not particularly in a fit of pique, but certainly with the attitude of 'If I'm not going to win, I'm not going to go on.' This was presented as the 'responsible' action to save the horse for the World Championships. The rumour turned to fact the following morning and left a disappointed atmosphere, not only among his legion of young fans who had come to watch their hero, but also with the organisation, who considered it a perhaps cavalier attitude to the privilege of riding at Badminton. Full credit to the sport becoming ever more professional, but where was sportsmanship? The delay in his official withdrawal also played havoc with the betting on the event.

We had some repercussions to this in the media centre, where one of my helpers, Becky, works as William's entry secretary. It was not the first nor last time in the horse world that conflicts of interest have arisen.

The world is full of 'ifs', but had Tamarillo stayed in the competition and gone clear inside the time, which 19 combinations managed to do, and show jumped clear, which six achieved, he would have finished third.

Ingrid Klimke for Germany led the first day of dressage on Sleep Late, but it is seldom that the first day leader isn't eclipsed on the Friday. She remained second with 40.4, but was pipped by Andrew Hoy on Sue Magnier's Moonfleet with a score of 36.5. Ruth and Terry were just behind them, joined by another second day combination, Ollie Townend with Flint Curtis who went into fifth on 43.5.

The previous autumn Zara Phillips had emulated her mother by becoming European Champion, with a storming round on Toy Town, in torrential rain, at Blenheim. She had yet to compete at Badminton, but the selectors wanted her to keep her powder dry for the 2006 World Championships at Aachen later in the year. We always look for an 'expert' to go round the course with Clare Balding for the TV preview. This is often quite difficult, since most of the 'names' will be riding.

The shelf life of riders seems to get longer and longer. My long-retired view is that the sport can't be as scary as it used to be, because any sane person would have lost their bottle a long time ago! Zara was our obvious choice. Unfortunately she wasn't over keen to do it, but we arranged that the crew would go round in one Mitsubishi, and I would chauffeur Clare, Zara and her England rugby international boyfriend Mike Tindall round to each location. Zara relaxed and Clare got some good footage.

During the event one of the grand ladies of the sport celebrated her 80th birthday. Jane (more familiarly known as Mrs) Rook is the widow of Laurence, former European Champion and Badminton winner in 1953. Laurence had also in his time been chairman of the sport in Britain, and one of the leading lights in its development. Jane herself was a familiar figure to riders of a certain age. She used to be a writer for the dressage judges, often the foreign ones, as she speaks several languages. She wore a cheery smile as we saluted, at the start and end of our tests. A gang of us were asked to her home, Beverstone Castle near Tetbury, where she threw a splendid party.

As ever Badminton was a marathon of intense hard work, intense socialising and unashamed networking. That year I welcomed into the media centre Princess Haya of Jordan, who had recently been elected as the President of the FEI (International Equestrian Federation), British Olympic chief, Lord Moynihan and Sports Minister Kate Hoey. The Princess is a former Olympic show jumper, and the other two have been to Badminton before, but we are always very proud to show people around the facilities. Unless people have been to Badminton they don't really understand the scale of the whole thing.

Hugh had set up a new warm-up area adjacent to the arena start area, where riders could have a pipe opener, jump some solid fences, or go for a decent spin up Worcester Avenue. First to go on Hugh's 32-fence course was Polly Stockton, who had experienced four-star short format the previous weekend in Kentucky. Her ride this time was Regulus. She jumped clear, but picked up some time penalties going the longer routes at a couple of fences.

The clears kept coming and coming, ending in 43 with a clean jumping sheet out of 53 finishers. Six retired and four were eliminated. If Hugh had erred on the cautious side for the first short year, it was probably a wise move. For the purists it was also a relief that good old fashioned thoroughbreds were still the right tools for the job.

Fourth overnight was Terry Boon and Foreign Exchange; up to third was Ollie Townend and Flint Curtis; second Ingrid Klimke, who was in the vanguard of German riders who were now capitalising on their usual superior dressage with matching flair across country. In pole position, however, was a rider whose quest for a win here after his Burghley title of 1979 had taken 27 years: Andrew Hoy.

On the Sunday morning Terry had to withdraw, but below him there wasn't a lot between eight of the potential placed horses. James Robinson (Commanche) and Jeanette Brakewell on the evergreen 18-year-old Over to You, which she would have retired had the format not changed, went clear to go up to fourth and fifth. Ollie's two down kept him in third, easing the pressure on the top two. Ingrid rolled one, but Hoy cruised round on Moonfleet to take the title with more than 10 penalties to spare.

It had been a good weekend for Sue Magnier, Moonfleet's owner. She couldn't be at Badminton because she was at Newmarket watching her 6–4 favourite George Washington come home by two and a half lengths in the 2000 Guineas.

To add to the excitement, Andrew had won Kentucky the week before, and amazingly the Rolex prize was in the offing again.

Andrew had become the oldest ever Badminton winner at 47,

overtaking Chris Bartle. This may support the theory of the ancient eventers, but at least there was some representative of youth at the sharp end. Ollie reminded the media at the final press conference that Andrew did his first Badminton four years before he was born.

After the official prize-giving, and the horses are back in the stable lines ready to go home, there is an indoor prize-giving, to present the replica trophies, special cups and other prizes in kind, such as saddles etc. to the successful riders. These extras are for categories such as best British rider, best rider on own horse, best rider to have never completed and even one presented by Lorna Clarke for the rider who pulls up the most places from an indifferent dressage. This used to be well away from the media as it happened in the sponsor's marquee. Now that the Mitsubishi hospitality is joined to the media centre we now have the final press conference which, when some champagne is served, turns into the final presentations. By definition, all those in the tent have had a good event, the media can mingle with the riders, and it all ends on a happy note.

Hard going

Over the summer Zara had indeed gone to Aachen and become World Champion with Toytown, so there was fevered speculation about her Badminton debut.

There had been a minor frenzy in 2004, when there had been a very outside possibility that she might go to the Athens Games. I had a fairly irritating spring, with both my Badminton and Olympic PR hats on as all anybody wanted was Zara stories. I, meanwhile, was fairly certain there wasn't one. British Eventing's PR department seemed keen for the myth to persist until I asked for clarification. The media could then concentrate on those who were going to Badminton and Athens.

This time, however, the interest was fully justified. Zara wasn't just of interest as tabloid fodder, but because she was reigning European and World Champion. To give her full due, she was up for interviews etc. if approached through the proper channels, like any top rider. She was also fairly unique in having gathered those two titles without yet trying the world's most testing event.

Needless to say I had loads of requests for her time. I filtered out the rankly stupid no-hopers, went through her official agents, but also had the back up of knowing the set-up at Gatcombe and her minders there. Though I had her number, it seemed much better to do it all officially. It was also of some help that Hugh Thomas happens to be one of her godfathers. It had been partly through his good offices that she had done the preview interviews the year before. I submitted a list of fairly sensible requests and had the OK to do children's programme BBC *Sportsround*, BBC West, ITV West and a Clare Balding interview for the main programme. The Chris Evans Radio 2 show was vetoed. (I put Ollie in to bat for that one.)

Three would be done after the riders' briefing on the Wednesday morning to get them out of the way, and Clare as early as possible.

I turned up as usual at the Badminton Village Hall for the rider briefing and spotted Zara and thanked her for agreeing to do the pieces and said I had a Shogun waiting to whisk her off to the shoots after the meeting. My three TV crews were there. She shook her head and said she knew nothing of any of this and had a dressage lesson with her stepmother Sandy in an hour. She hadn't been at Gatcombe for over a week and had no idea what had been agreed in her name. So much for going through the proper channels!

She said she would do the children's programme and the others would have to wait. After lunch the two crews set up in front of the house and I went down to the horsebox lines to drive her up to the park. She would prefer if they came down to her. Down yomped the presenters and crew. BBC West got theirs in the bag. It was then ITV's turn. Jed the reporter wondered if Z might remove her riding hat because of the shadow.

'Erm no.'

'Why not?'

'Because my hair . . . it looks . . . it looks . . . well it looks like Julian's.'

Good enough excuse, I'd say.

The atmosphere at the event, however, was to become something less than light-hearted. When the riders had first had a look at the course, they were very concerned at the state of the going. It had been a very dry spring, and the expected rain had not fallen the previous week.

What had been billed as a high-class field was in danger of being decimated by withdrawls. The rout was British led. Mary King pulled out her two: Cashel Bay and Call Again Cavalier. Up and coming prospects Ollie Townend, Daisy Dick and Sharon Hunt kept Flint Curtis, Springalong and Tankers Town in their stables, and the final blow to the media machine was the withdrawal of Toytown and Zara, who were lying in sixth after the dressage.

There was then an enormous and overnight damage limitation exercise, with tons of topsoil being laid along the whole length of the course under the auspices of the technical delegate, Mike Etherington-Smith. Germany's team trainer, Britain's Chris Bartle, pretty well kept walking the course from the early hours before sanctioning his charges to compete if they wanted to. In the event 22 didn't want to take the risk and most of them were British.

An understandably nervous Hugh said he didn't know if there would be as many as 50 not willing to go.

On Saturday morning there was a defiant air about those who had decided to run. Kim Severson, the multiple Kentucky winner and Olympic silver medallist from the USA, had said that she was used to similar going in the States and was not worried. Lucinda Fredericks, born British but married Australian and adopting her new country's can-do attitude, was already the dressage leader with Headley Britannia. If she was going to win Badminton this would be the year, and if some of her serious challengers didn't want to take her on, that was their problem.

When things aren't going your way, they just don't. Daisy Dick was first to go on her other horse, only to fall at the penultimate fence, the Rolex Turn. The fence was removed thereafter. The first element of The Quarry had been taken out before the cross country started. These cuts didn't help the system of achieving time penalties, as one horse Air Jordan 2 and Frank Ostholt for Germany, was 17 seconds inside the time.

The familiar Vicarage Vee penalised four of the runners, but was also the scene of one of those freak accidents, which no one could have predicted in more than 55 years of jumping round Badminton. Icare D'Auzay, the mount of Frenchman Jean Lou Bigot, hung badly to the right over the rail corner over the ditch, snapping the flag stick, which then stuck in the ground. The horse then staked itself on this, in the groin. Despite instant veterinary care, and subsequent transfer to a specialist centre, the horse couldn't be saved. The whole incident held up the course for 40 minutes. Wooden flag posts had never been seen as dangerous, but once proved to be a potential hazard, albeit by a freak accident, they would not be used again.

This was hard for the riders out on the course, not least Jonty Evans, who was suffering from muscle spasms from an injury incurred shortly before Badminton, but also for the BBC and their new director, Jerry Morrison, who had an eon of dead time to fill. Whatever the BBC pay Clare Balding, it isn't enough. She was quite brilliant at finding fillers. The problem did however expose the, perhaps worth it, risks of covering eventing live on mainstream weekend sports TV.

There had also been another fatality, when the 15-year-old Skwal died of a heart attack after completing the course.

All of what had happened throughout the week, whether culpable or bad luck, was of course played out in the glare of publicity. As Media Officer, my job is to promote the event and secure the best possible publicity. When it goes wrong, the Media Officer is naturally somewhat exposed. If we had lost the goodwill of the riders as early as Wednesday, we had probably lost the media by Thursday. What happened on the Saturday, which had nothing to do with the accepted disaster of the going, just added to the woes.

In reality, the Herculean efforts of the ground team had in fact made the course quite rideable, and a rather exciting competition unfolded. As Lucinda Fredericks said as she completed: 'I was pleasantly surprised how well the ground rode.'

With the effective walkout of the British contingent, 12 of the top 13 were from other countries, with the exception of Sarah Cohen, who ran and came ninth with Hide and Seek II.

Lucinda Fredericks was a worthy winner with Headley Britannia, having led from the front, and can therefore be happy in the knowledge that she wasn't the winner only because someone better hadn't run. This, fortuitously, genuinely managed to maintain the prestige of the Mitsubishi title. Andreas Dibowski from Germany was second with FRH Serve Well, and third was the USA's Kim Severson, who of course, had given the going her positive vote well before the cross country. Meanwhile Andrew Nicholson had notched up 25 comple-tions, this time with Lord Killinghurst and Henry Tankerville, both placed. By now his sideboard army of silver replicas of the main trophy must have overtaken the Gatcombe display of the 1980s.

In a very short period, probably less than three years, the whole nature of the sport of Three Day Eventing had both undergone a seismic change in adopting the short format, and also revealed a change in attitudes, which might have been latent, but came to the fore in 2007. The new reality was:

99 per cent of riders at Badminton level were professional.

The value of a Badminton-level horse was in six figures.

Ergo they wouldn't be risked on questionable going.

The prize money was no longer 'token', but valuable.

Short format made it possible to run top horses many more times a year and was here to stay.

Any minor impediment to the big prize would justify retiring at any stage, to go again next week.

Because of their professional status, competitive riders were staying in the saddle much longer, and had long since stopped being intimidated by 'elders and betters' who had been there before.

In a litigious and media-dominated society, Health and Safety and image considerations had to be taken into account.

While Hugh admitted openly at the start of Badminton 2007 that he was 'Not proud' of the going, and by any criteria it was too hard, it became apparent that only golf course fairway conditions were adequate at this level of the sport. (Just to stay with the golf analogy for a second, the American golf stars have had to deal with our Links courses to win The Open, the sport's top prize. The main section of eventing was supposed to be natural cross country, but I digress.)

Over the autumn of 2007 a massive ground improvement plan was put into action. The results of this ongoing project were seen as early as the October of the year. The only foreseeable downside to this was that the route, whether clock- or anticlockwise, would now be set in turf, perhaps forever. Perhaps never again would riders venture over the Luckington Lane.

Onwards and upwards

Very much in keeping with equestrian tradition, the best thing to do after a fall is to get straight back into the saddle and go again. The build up to Badminton 2008 was incredibly positive. The turf management was paying visible dividends. The equestrian world acknowledged that enormous efforts were being made to make the going more than acceptable to the sensibilities for the 21st century version of a 19th century concept.

In October 2007 Hugh invited various interested parties, including riders and trainers, to see the work in progress on the ground. In the spring the Duke asked me to suggest some media people he might ask for lunch and a preview of the new greensward that was the route of the course.

As an organisation, Badminton knew it had to get itself back on track. It had easily absorbed the short format formula. Indeed the changeover had been surprisingly easy, which the sceptics had to concede. But 2007 needed exorcising.

Hugh and the office had their work to do, and media wise I also had some catching up to do.

On a practical level, I had some changes to take on board:

The whole media centre and Mitsubishi Motors Hospitality was to move to a different spot on the site. The old area, in view of the House, had ruined the grass underneath the tentage, and after decades of use the Duke wanted it to recover.

Gabi had left Mitsubishi and her assistant Nic was on maternity leave, so I had a new team to ease into the idiosyncrasies of my operation.

My accreditation system went digital for the first time.

My computer died in March.

The new database was infested by gremlins, so accessing info for the biographies was a nightmare.

The boss of Mitsubishi rejigged the entire Hospitality/Media tentage on the Wednesday before the Event.

As it turned out, we were all ready, as ever, to get the whole thing going.

In the run up I had the standard requests for interviews etc., but one of the increasingly tricky ones is to suggest a past rider to do the *Horse & Hound* course walk. As I have mentioned before, most of the old riders are still at it, and Ginny, Lucinda and Ian have done the job so often that the magazine understandably was keen on a new voice. I mooted a former European, World and Olympic gold medallist, albeit from some years ago, who was also a journalist . . .

H&H: 'No, our readers won't remember . . . and we need a glam youngster to sell copies.'

JS: 'How about a top show jumping lady rider to compare disciplines?'

H&H: 'Yes, but no.'

I kept ringing Hugh with possible ideas, and then came up with what I thought was a perfect amalgam of a celebrity equestrian who could sell copies. (I didn't at this stage alert H&H.) 'Hugh,' I emailed, 'I give you Katie Price, aka Jordan'. Two seconds later I had an email reply: 'Julian, now I know you have lost it.'

It wasn't until our TV meeting, some weeks before the event, that Hugh became fully conversant with the equestrian oeuvre of Ms Price. The answer was still no! Luckily Jeanette Brakewell was not entered for the first time in ages, and was the perfect choice. . . But . . . but . . .

The smart press lunch on Thursday in the sponsor's area had been a welcome media treat for many years. The format was simple. The media arrived and were offered a drink, lunch places were bagged on

MITSUBISHI MOTORS
BADMINTON HORSE TRIALS 2008
32
MITSUBISHI MOTORS
M
MITSUBISHI MOTORS
BADMINTON HORSE TRIALS
1 – 4 May 2008
Price £5.00
MITSUBISHI MOTORS

an ad hoc basis, and Hugh would introduce proceedings, hand over to the Managing Director of Mitsubishi Motors for a few words, and then I would welcome the press. After the previous year this was rather crucial.

Hugh had a different idea now: Julian to introduce, Mitsubishi, then Hugh. No problem. I had asked the top MM man, whom I had known for seven years, what 'title' he wanted to be introduced as. MD would be fine.

The assembled press were happily seated as I took the microphone. Welcome . . . blah . . . blah. . . . And I have pleasure in introducing you to the Managing Director of Mitsubishi Motors . . . (senior moment . . . silence) . . . (stage whisper from himself) . . . (confident delivery) . . . Jim Tyrrell. . . . No one was fooled.

BBC News, their 24 hour service, had expressed an interest to film from Badminton. They were after a 'magazine' type overview of the Event. Their presenter was Nick Higham. By fabulous coincidence the very camera friendly, long-time stud groom at Badminton was his namesake, Brian Higham. Brian did a fantastic piece to camera in the stable yard, 'live' on Saturday morning, including a tour of the fabulous 18th century tack room.

The 2008 course headed left-handed to The Quarry, now, so early in the track, a fairly welcoming combination of big logs and slopes. Huntsman's Close hosted a corner option that would require serious steering through the trees and The Lake came quite early at fences eight and nine.

Most fences now required pinpoint accuracy, rather than bravado, and Ian Stark's 10-year-old observation had been realised: Grade A show jumping Gymkhana ponies were the ticket. There were choices at the Blue Cross Round Tops, the City Farm Complex, the Colt Pond, the Hexagon Hedge (Vicarage Vee), the old Irish Bank, the Shogun Hollow, the Staircase, and the house jumps at the Lancer Village.

In another Olympic year there were riders of all nationalities staking their claim. The winner, however, was the first 'continental' rider since Hans Schwarzenbach to take the Badminton title, Nicholas Touzaint, for France on Hildago de L'ille. So close behind was Lucy Wiegersma (the nine-year-old winner of my Alvin Stardust gig in 1990) with Shaabrak.

It was a perfect course for the sport in the new era, which had been through some genuinely hard years of decision making. Twenty-eight jumped round clear, but only two made the time. The French win was supported by a superbly vociferous Gallic fan club.

The sport had shaken itself into the modern world, and Badminton, with all its history, was as ever, its pinnacle.

END PIECE

Badminton is an entity in itself, which has developed incredibly since its inception as a schooling set up for British Olympic success. Almost from the beginning it has been the major event of its type in the world. The first crowd of 6,000 has now grown to almost 200,000 over the weekend.

The early competitors were mature equestrians from hunting and military backgrounds. When the sport progressed, younger riders emerging from the Pony Club and then the junior and Young Rider ranks were up for the challenge. For many years most riders were amateurs and moved on in their mid-20s.

The sport and Badminton have constantly evolved over the years. Sometimes the changes and tweaks have been instigated by major events and sometimes dictated by ruling bodies, both national and international. Show jumping penalties have come down from 10 to five (1979) and now four (2003). Going very fast cross country ceased to give riders bonus points. If the horse falls now they are eliminated. The final run-in phase was abolished. Roads and tracks and steeplechase were abolished in 2006. A minimum weight for riders was phased out in 1998. A horse 'aspirin' drug called Bute was banned in 1992.

Over 60 years all of these changes have subtly changed the emphasis of the sport, but because they have been gradual' neither the public nor to some extent the riders have experienced a sudden change, apart perhaps from the introduction of the short format in 2006.

One or two of the middle-era riders decided that they were to become 'Professional Eventers', a term once as contradictory as 'Military Intelligence'. But they stayed the course and most continued for many years.

Over 60 years Badminton has provided a superb number of talking points, and every year brings a new story, theory and often a challenge to any received wisdom.

Here are 20 round-up facts from the preceding pages:

Richard Walker was the youngest winner at 18, Andrew Hoy the oldest at 47.

Director Hugh Thomas came second at the event, in 1976, and so did the current Duke, David Somerset, in 1959.

Lucinda Green won on six different horses, Be Fair, Wideawake, George, Killaire, Regal Realm and Beagle Bay.

Richard Meade lost it once on time penalties, when last to go in the show jumping.

Bill Roycroft and Lorna Clarke (Sutherland) were the only two riders to go round three times in one day.

Badminton was a One Day Event in 1963 because of the weather.

Badminton was cancelled in 1966 and 1987 because of the weather, and abandoned after the dressage in 1975. In 2001 it didn't take place because of the foot and mouth outbreak.

Badminton made a profit of £20.00 in its first year.

There have been five directors: Trevor Horn, Gordon Cox-Cox, David Somerset, Frank Weldon and Hugh Thomas.

In 1955, by invitation of the Queen, Badminton, as European Championships, was run at Windsor.

The competition has been won by four Australians: Bill Roycroft, Laurie Morgan, Andrew Hoy and Lucinda Fredericks (by marriage); two Irish: Mark Darley and Eddie Boylan; two Americans: Bruce Davidson and David O'Connor; one Swiss: Hans Schwarzenbach, one New Zealander: Mark Todd (three times); and one Frenchman: Nicolas Touzaint.

Badminton used to be run in April but moved to May in 1988. The weather has been equally fickle since.

Roads and tracks and steeplechase were abolished from 2006.

From 1959 to 1965 there were two sections, Great Badminton and Little Badminton.

The synonymous shuttlecock game was invented in Badminton's front Hall.

Badminton has enjoyed two of sport's longest-lasting sponsorships: Whitbread from 1961 to 1991 and Mitsubishi Motors from 1992.

With increasing crowds it was decided to run the cross country on the Friday in 1974. This unpopular departure was put right when the event returned after the abandonment of 1975.

The Poacher is the only horse to have won Little Badminton (with his owner Martin Whiteley in 1965) and Great Badminton (with Richard Meade in 1970).

Badminton was the second Three Day Event to be run in Great Britain. The first was its inspiration, the 1948 Olympics.

The maximum dimensions of the fences have not changed since 1912.

Badminton Horse Trials has been a very important part of many people's lives, including my own. It has gone through many changes, but the essence of the challenge remains. It has become one of the nation's big family outings, even for those with only a passing interest in horses. The nuances of change may exercise the minds of those of us intimately involved in the sport, but almost certainly not have been noticed by the majority of visitors over the years. And as Col. Weldon used to say: 'It is their day out.'

Badminton is so much more than 'The Most Important Horse Event in Great Britain.' That was in 1949.